Four Women Poets

Edited by Judith Baxter

CAMBRIDGE
UNIVERSITY PRESS

The publishers would like to thank Nicholas McGuinn and
Jane Ogborn for their help as consulting editors for the series.

Published by the Press Syndicate of the University of Cambridge
The Pitt Building, Trumpington Street, Cambridge CB2 1RP
40 West 20th Street, New York, NY 10011-4211, USA
10 Stamford Road, Oakleigh, Melbourne 3166, Australia

Selection and notes © Cambridge University Press 1995

First published 1995

Printed in Great Britain by Scotprint, Musselburgh, Scotland

A catalogue record for this book is available from the British Library

ISBN 0 521 48545 2 paperback

Prepared for publication by Stenton Associates

Cover photographs: Fleur Adcock courtesy of Oxford University Press;
Liz Lochhead courtesy of Network Photographers Ltd; Jackie Kay
courtesy of Ingrid Pollard, Bloodaxe Books; Carol Ann Duffy courtesy
of Sue Adler of the *Observer*.

Thanks are due to the following for permission to reproduce poems:
pp. 10–24 from *Bagpipe Muzak* by Liz Lochhead reproduced by
permission of Penguin Books Ltd © Liz Lochhead, 1991; pp. 26–32
from *True Confessions / Dreaming Frankenstein* by Liz Lochhead
reproduced by permission of Polygon; p. 34 *The Adoption Papers* by
Jackie Kay, 1991 reproduced by permission of Bloodaxe Books Ltd;
pp. 60–66 *Standing Female Nude* by Carol Ann Duffy, published in
1985; pp. 67–76 *The Other Country* by Carol Ann Duffy, published in
1990; pp. 77–84 *Mean Time* by Carol Ann Duffy, published in 1993
by Anvil Press Poetry; pp. 86–108 reprinted from Fleur Adcock's
Selected Poems (1983) and from *The Incident Book* by Fleur Adcock
(1986) by permission of Oxford University Press. Every attempt has
been made to locate copyright for all the material in this book. The
publishers would be glad to hear from anyone whose copyright has
been unwittingly infringed.

CONTENTS

CAMBRIDGE LITERATURE

Four Women Poets is part of the Cambridge Literature series, and has been specially prepared for students in schools and colleges who are studying the book as part of their English course.

This study edition invites you to think about what happens when you read a poem, and it suggests that you are not passively responding to words on the page which have only one agreed interpretation, but that you are actively exploring and making new sense of what you read. Your 'reading' will partly stem from you as an individual, from your own experiences and point of view, and to this extent your interpretation will be distinctively your own. But your reading will also stem from the fact that you belong to a culture and a community, rooted in a particular time and place. So, your understanding may have much in common with that of others in your class or study group.

There is a parallel between the way you read these poems and the way they were written. The Resource Notes at the back are devised to help you to investigate the complex nature of the writing process. This begins with the poets' first, tentative ideas and sources of inspiration, moves through to the stages of writing, production and publication, and ends with the text's reception by the reading public, reviewers, critics and students. So the general approach to study focuses on five key questions:

Who has written these poems and why?

What type of texts are they?

How were they produced?

How do they present their subject?

Who reads them? How do they interpret them?

The text of *Four Women Poets* is presented complete and uninterrupted. You will find some words in the text asterisked: these are words which may be unfamiliar because they have a particular cultural or linguistic significance. They are explained in the Glossary section at the back.

The Resource Notes encourage you to take an active and imaginative approach to studying poetry both in and out of the classroom. As well as providing you with information about many aspects of *Four Women Poets* they offer a wide choice of activities to work on individually, or in groups. Above all, they give you the chance to explore this anthology in a variety of ways: as a reader, an actor, a researcher, a critic and a writer.

Judith Baxter, Series Editor

4

THE POEMS

INTRODUCTION

In this collection of poetry and performance pieces, you will hear many voices – both the apparent and implied voices of the four poets, and also the carnival of characters who speak through their work: the powerful and the weak; the exotic and the homely; the serious and the absurd. Many of the characters are searching for a better understanding of their identity, by questioning the roles they are expected to play, or the labels they must conform to.

If there is a common link between the writings in this collection, it is this – the concern with human identity. All four poets explore the shifting, complex nature of what it is to be human, and how easy it is to be labelled, stereotyped, misinterpreted, miscast and misunderstood.

One labelling this text uses is implied in the title, *Four Women Poets*. Of the four, not all would classify themselves exclusively as 'poets': Liz Lochhead, for example, is noted as much for her plays and humorous recitations as for her poems, and this collection includes examples of her performance pieces. Jackie Kay has written a novel and several plays, and, indeed, *The Adoption Papers* has been recorded as a radio play. You might consider this question as you read: is the boundary between, say, a poem and a dramatic monologue always clear and distinct? Or are the boundaries between the literary genres fluid and contestable?

As women, these poets do indeed have powerful and challenging things to say about gender, and this kind of social critique may be an essential part of their work. They also believe in representing the female voice in their work, but none of the four are typecast by this. Fleur Adcock believes in the value of women's poetry anthologies, but objects to their being placed in the 'women's sections' of bookshops. Carol Ann Duffy has said, 'I don't mind being called a feminist poet but I wouldn't mind if I wasn't. I think the concerns of art go beyond that.' Liz Lochhead acknowledges the male and female presence in all writers, whatever their gender. Jackie Kay believes that what you write is important, not the label you use. In a recent interview she commented:

> I think all these long lists after your name, being Scottish, feminist, vegetarian, socialist, it gets a bit much! I write directly from my own experience; people do get a sense of the multiplicity of what I am.

The Resource Notes at the back of this book encourage you to consider the multiple, and distinctive voices of each poet in the collection. Your own views and responses are very important here too. Traditionally, students of literature have been taught various ways of reading and responding to poems, some of which were considered more 'correct' than others. In contrast, the Resource Notes encourage you to read, perform and interpret the poems in differing ways, and from varying points of view. They also ask you to consider how individual readings of poems are intimately bound up with issues of identity – who we are, and what kind of culture we live in. The notion, therefore, of a 'correct' reading of a poem is something you may wish to question.

These four poets offer something different from the mainstream literary tradition. Until recently, school poetry anthologies were dominated by the words of established writers, who were usually white, anglo-saxon, male and preferably dead. This collection is not unique in offering an alternative to that tradition, but what it hopes to do is to represent the diverse and contrasting experiences that have been articulated in poetry, by four widely acclaimed women.

Judith Baxter

Liz Lochhead

Almost Miss Scotland

The night I
Almost became Miss Scotland,
I caused a big stramash°
When I sashayed on in my harristweed heathermix onepiece
And my 'Miss Garthamlock' sash.   5

I wis six-fit-six, I wis slinky
(Yet nae skinnymalinky°) –
My waist was nipped in wi elastic,
My powder and panstick were three inches thick,
Nails? Long, blood-rid and plastic.   10
So my big smile'd come across, I'd larded oan lipgloss
And my false eyelashes were mink
With a sky blue crescent that was pure iridescent
When I lowered my eyelids to blink.

Well, I wiggled tapselteerie,° my heels were that peerie°   15
While a kinna Jimmy Shandish band
Played 'Flower of Scotland' –
But it aw got droont oot wi wolf whistles –
And that's no countin 'For These Are My Mountains'
– See I'd tits like nuclear missiles.   20

Then this familiar-lukkin felly
I'd seen a loat oan the telly
Interviewed me aboot my hobbies –
I says: Macrame, origami,
Being nice tae my mammy –   25
(Basically I tellt him a loat o jobbies).
I was givin it that
Aboot my ambition to chat
To handicapped and starvin children from other nations
– How I was certain I'd find   30

Travel wid broaden my mind
As I fulfilled my Miss Scotland obligations.

Well, I wis in Seventh Heaven
To be in the Final Seven –
But as the Judges retired   35
To do what was required
And pick the furst, second and thurd
Well, the waiting was murder and it suddenly occurred there
Was something *absurd*
Aboot the hale position   40
Of being in competition
Wi other burds like masel
Who I should of kennt very well
Were ma sisters (at least under the skin)
Yet fur this dubious prize I'd have scratched oot their eyes 45
And hoped they'd git *plooks*,° so I'd win!
Aye, there wis somethin ridic'lous
Boot sookin in wi thae prickless
Wonders o judges, their 'winks' and their 'nudges'.
Wan wee baldy comedian bloke   50
Whose jokes were a joke:
Wan heuchter-choochter° singer who wis a dead ringer
For a cross between a pig in a tartan poke
And a constipated bubblyjock:°
Plus wan wellknown soak –   55
A member of our Sporting Fraternity
Who was guaranteed his place in Eternity
As a well-pickled former member of the Scotland Squad.
And the likes of them were Acting God,
Being Real Men,   60
Scoring *us* on a scale of one to ten –
They'd compare and contrast, and then at last
They'd deign to pronounce
And reverse-order-announce it.
Then I wid simper, look sweet, an   65
I'd burst oot greetin
Gasp 'Who me' – the usual story –

They'd plonk me down, stick on the Miss Scotland crown
To crown my crowning glory.

How would *thae guys* like to be a prize –   70
A cake everybody wanted a slice of –
Have every leering schoolgirl consider them a pearl
Everybody kennt the price of?
How would *they* like their mums to say that their bums
Had always attracted the Ladies' Glances,   75
And nothing wrang wi it, they'd aye gone alang wi it
And encouraged them to take their chances?
And they were Good Boys, their Mum's Pride & Joys,
Saving it for their Future Wives?
And despite their fame they still steyed at hame   80
And lived real clean-living lives?

In a blinding flash I saw the hale thing was trash
– I just Saw Rid
And here's whit I did

– Now I'd love to report that I was the sort   85
To speak out and convince the other lassies
Pick bones wi aw the chaperones
And singlehandedly convert the masses
Till in a bacchanalian Revenge of the Barbie Dolls
Crying 'All for One and One for All!'   90
We advanced on the stage, full of bloodlust and rage –
But, I cannot tell a lie, the truth is that I
Just stuck on my headsquerr and snuck away oot o therr –
I know I did right, it wisnae contrary –
And I let my oaxters° grow back in   95
Really rid and thick and hairy.

Because the theory of feminism's aw very well
But yiv got tae see it fur yirsel
Every individual hus tae realize
Her hale fortune isnae in men's eyes,   100
Say enough is enough
Away and get stuffed.

Meeting Norma Nimmo

Hello, hello, it is you, isn't it?

I thought it was.

My, I haven't seen you since school. I have not
clepped eyes on you since the Sixth Year Leavers' Social. I
mind of you diving around in bleck tights and a big   5
fisherman's jumper shoogling up esperins in Coca-Cola
and eating the insides of Vick inhalers trying to get stoned.

You've not changed.

Not really, well, putting on the beef a bit but who
hasnae!   10

Listen ... listen, do you mind Joyce Kirdie? Mind,
reddish hair, freckles, was always a hoot in the French
class, did dentistry?

She killed herself.

No, no epperently she wasn't depressed. No, I asked   15
her sister at the funeral, but no, it's a mystery ... Order in
for Liberty curtains, booked up for three weeks in the
nice bit of Ibeetha, own Lawrence-home in Kirkie, rubber
tube on the exhaust of her H-reg and hallelujah.

Her mother was devastated. Looked about one   20
hundred and five. Mark you, I call it the coward's way
out ...

Do you know who I ren into outside the
crematorium? Moira Lennox. Epperently she'd bumped
into Merjorie Sneddon. You do mind Merjorie! She won   25
the Mysie Thomson Inglis prize for Excellence in Art
three years hard running but wisnae allowed to go to the
Art School because her mother was a Plymouth Brethren?

EEC. Brussels. Bilingual private secretary to some
bigwig, fabulous selery, she loved the lifestyle. Moira said 30
a week later she was dead, choked on a truffle ...

Mind you, poor Moira has been having her own share
of troubles recently. Ocht, aye you do mind Moira
Lennox. Big fet lassie, brilliant at *Letin*. Well, epperently,
she joined the Scotstoun branch of the Society of Serious   35
Slimmers and ended up semi-enorexic.

Oh, wait till I tell you … Rosamund Petterson.
Blondish, right sexpot, used to go out with the Glesgow
Ecedemy School Ceptain … Modelled briefly. Then she
married one of the Everage White Band. Or wis it mibbe   40
the Marmalade? Anyhow, she emigrated with him to Bel
Air, he divorced her for Rod Stewart's ex and she ended
up with a drug dependency problem living with some
elcoholic screen-writer who tried to strengle her to death
in a drunken rage. Well, he could efford the good lawyer   45
so he ended up getting off with the ettempted murder
charge plus she lost custody of the children.

She's beck home now, running a wee
knitwear-and-yarns shop in Clerkston.

Anyway I'm going out with her for a wee G. and T.   50
on Gordie's squash night. She'll be *fes*cinated that I met
you …

The Complete
Alternative History of the World,
Part One

There was this man alone
In a beautiful garden.
Stark bollock naked
(Scuse my French, beg your pardon)

He was, yes, the original Nature's Gentleman.   5
He was in tune, at one, with nature
And the lion lay down with the lamb,
Each peaceable creature
Knew its place in the Order of Things
(And if God meant men to be angels   10
He'd have given them wings).

The climate was brilliant
The weather was sunny
The whole land flowed with
Milk and honey   15
Soothing fragrant grasses
Waved verdant in the breeze
Breadfruit baked itself in the sun
And fell out of the trees
Where, by the way, songbirds were singing   20
With bees for a backing
– Oh a right bed of roses!
But there was Something Lacking ...
He couldny put his finger on it,
He was in a right tizz.   25
But, the Lord Our God being a Male God,
He knew exactly whit it wis ...

A slave.

And soon she was worn to a frazzle
Waiting on His Nibs   30
Ironing his figleaves
Barbecueing his ribs
While home came the hunter
With the Bacon for the table
She was stuck raising Cain   35
And breastfeeding Abel.
Him: The Big Breid-winner
Her: A Machine for breedin'
Barescud and pregnant?
Some Garden of Eden!   40
The sort of sexist division of labour
That went out with the Ark –
i.e. the nuclear family –
Bugger that for a Lark.

So they were both Ripe for Revolting   45
When that Slimy Serpent came
But – would you Adam and Eve it? –
She got the blame.

She could've saved us all a whole lot of trouble if only   50
she'd told him right at the start:

I'm not your Little Woman
I'm not your Better Half
I'm not your nudge, your snigger
Or your belly laugh.

I'm not Jezebel°   55
And I'm not Delilah°
I'm not Mary Magdalen°
Or the Virgin Mary either.

Not a Novice or a Nun
Nor a Hooker or a Stripper   60
Not Super Shirley Conran
Not Jill the Ripper.

No I'm no Scissor-Lady –
I won't snip at your ... locks.
I'm not a siren,° you're not obliged   65
To get off my rocks.

Not Medusa,° not Medea°
And, though my tongue may be salty,
I'm not the Delphic sybil° –
Or Sybil Fawlty.   70

I'm not Poison Ivy
You can throw away the lotion
I'm not your Living Doll
I'm not Poetry In Motion.

And if selling Booze and Cars   75
Involves my body being used, well ...
I'm not Queen Victoria
But I'm not amused.

And if you don't like my Body
You can sodding well lump it –   80
I'm not a Tart-with-a-Golden-Heart
Or Thinking Man's Crumpet.

I'm not your Woman of Achievement
Not your Slimmer of the Year
I'm not Princess Diana ...   85
No Frog Princes 'ere!

I'm not little Ms Midler
I'm not little Miss Muffet
Make me An Offer I Can't Refuse –
And I'll tell you to stuff it!   90

'Cos I'm not your Little Woman
I'm not your Lady Wife
I'm not your Old Bag
Or the Love of Your Life –

No, I'm not your Little Woman   95
Not your Better Half
I'm not your Nudge, your Snigger
Or your Belly Laugh.

Con-densation

After two and a half years with His Mother
We were no longer love's young dream
When me, him and the weans got a hoose o' wur ain
In a four-in-a-block in this scheme.

But – somewhat to our disappointment –   5
When we turned the key in the door
It was Very Sanderson, very substandard,
When it came to the décor.

Telltale black marks roon the cooker and sink,
Toadstools on the ceiling   10
And the back bedroom was boggin' wi' damp
(It gave you a clammy feeling).

Plus the bathroom had been invaded
By a sortofa fungussy thing
That looked quite a lot like it was part of a plot   15
From a horrorbook by Stephen King.

Of course we complained.
We complained again. And – eventually – the Corporation
Sent a couple of fellas who were quick to tell us
'If it's any consolation   20
The water that's runnin' down your walls
Isn't dampness, it's con-densation.'

'Oh,' says I, 'I see,' says I,
'Whit's that when it's at hame?'
Seems dampness comes in, oot the ootside,   25
But if it's condensation we're to blame.

Well, taking baths in the bathroom
Or boiling kettles in the kitchenette
Or shutting-up windaes in winter to keep the heat in
Or warming up rooms with paraffin   30
It all causes steam, don't forget.

Well, pardon us for breathing, (I was really seething)
We complained again. Then complained-again again.
The woman said, 'Now please don't be abusive
I can assure you you've nothing to gain.'   35

She came she saw she tutted.
She said, 'I see what you mean …
Yon's murder on your Laura Ashley
And it's awfully hard to keep clean.'

She was very sympathetic   40
I have to admit she was *nice*.
But short of hopin' we'd keep the windaes wide open
And the fire oan full blast
And breathe shallow and fast
She was very short of advice.   45

Well, it's the same the whole world over
It's the poor what gets the blame
And the rich that gets the … central heating.
Isn't that a blooming shame?

Well, what do we expect with this Government's   50
Distribution of wealth –
They wish to get back to Victorian Values
And Dickensian Standards of Health.

View of Scotland / Love Poem

Down on her hands and knees
at ten at night on Hogmanay,◊
my mother still giving it elbowgrease
jiffywaving the vinolay. (This is too
ordinary to be nostalgia.) On the kitchen table   5
a newly opened tin of sockeye◊ salmon.
Though we do not expect anyone,
the slab of black bun,
petticoat-tails fanned out
on bone china.   10
'Last year it was very quiet ...'

Mum's got her rollers in with waveset
and her well-pressed good dress
slack across the candlewick upstairs.
Nearly half-ten already and her not shifted!   15
If we're to even hope to prosper
this midnight must find us
how we would like to be.
A new view of Scotland
with a dangling calendar   20
is propped under last year's,
ready to take its place.

Darling, it's thirty years since
anybody was able to trick me,
December thirtyfirst, into   25
'looking into a mirror to see a lassie
wi' as minny heids as days in the year' –
and two already since,
familiar strangers at a party,
we did not know that we were   30

21

the happiness we wished each other
when the Bells went, did we?

All over the city
off-licences pull down their shutters.
People make for where they want to be   35
to bring the new year in.
In highrises and tenements
sunburst clocks tick
on dusted mantelshelves.
Everyone puts on their best spread of plenty   40
(for to even hope to prosper
this midnight must find us
how we would like to be).
So there's a bottle of sickly liqueur
among the booze in the alcove,   45
golden crusts on steak pies
like quilts on a double bed.
And this is where we live.
There is no time like the
present for a kiss.   50

Renfield's Nurse

When I go in to him
I never know what to expect.
I move in antiseptic corridors.
I come bearing a bedpan like a begging bowl.
I bring hot water, carbolic, huckaback.◇   5
I bring a hypodermic, a bowl
of brown stew I've saved for him special,
or three dicey horse pills
rattling like chance in a plastic cup.

Times   10
he'll be nice as ninepence
sitting up smiling
that pink and bland you'd
swear he'd all his marbles.
Lucid as the next man.   15

Others
when he doesn't know me from Adam –
though he's always got a glad eye for the girls.
I blame the uniform.

Sometimes   20
he cowers in his own dirt in the corner
whimpering
Doctor don't you hurt me Doctor.
I say it's just the nurse
I say come on you know it's only me.   25
He looks up at me
with them dog eyes and says
you the nice one or the nasty 'cause I never
know what to expect?

My hands are gentle.   30
My starched apron cracks
like a whip hand.

Good Wood

hardwood
softwood.
sapwood
heartwood.
firewood   5
dyestuffs coal and amber.
bowls broomhandles platters textile rollers
maple sycamore wildcherry gean.◇
paperpulp brushbacks besomheads horsejumps
birch.   10
alder clogs a certain special charcoal
used in the manufacture of gunpowder.
spindles. dogwood skewers.
cricket bats fine willow charcoal for artists' use.
hornbeam oxyokes   15
mallets cogs and butchers' chopping blocks.
walnut gunstocks
tableware veneered interiors.
poplar and aspen woodwool
chipbaskets matchsticks and matchboxes.   20
chestnut hop poles posts and stakes.
blackthorn walkingsticks
the traditional shillelagh.◇
wattle wattlehurdles
peasticks beanrods heathering hazel-withes and hoops.   25
ash tennis
racquets billiard cues and hockey sticks.
holly for turnery inlaid work and marquetry.◇
larch planking.
linden hatblocks and pianokeys.   30
grand fir noble fir douglas fir spruce cypress pine
pitprops paperpulp packing cases

roofing flooring railway sleepers and telegraph poles.
bathtime fragrances of cedarwood and sandalwood.
oak tanning pigmast panelling   35
and scottish fishing craft.
elmwood coffins in damp earth might warp won't split.

Six Men Monologues

No. 1: Annemarie.

Men see men I've had it
Up to here absolutely
It's all off completely.
I said suppose that'll suit you fine I said
You can go out with your mates   5
Every night of the week and not just Thursdays
I said,
Look at the state of you
The beer's all going to your belly already
And coming from the West of Scotland you   10
Are statistically unlikely
even to reach the age of 25
without false teeth
And to tell the truth
Since we got engaged   15
You never bother with the Brut
or the good suit I said
I'm sick to the backteeth of
Every time we go for a Chinese
You order   20
chicken and chips, fried egg and peas.
I said No way
Believe me the only way I'd ever consider
The World Cup in Mala-bloody-ga
For my honeymoon   25
Is if I was guaranteed
An instant trade you in for a
Six foot shit-hot sharp shooter that never failed to hit the spot.
I told him where to stick his bloody
One carrot diamond-is-forever.   30

I blame his mother.

No. 2: Pamela.

Men, my boyfriend says, Honest-to-God he says men
huvn't got it any easier than women these days! He says
men aren't any more sure and secure within their own
sexual identity. Oh naw, not by a long, long chalk. And   35
yiv got tae watch not tae laugh at them, huvn't yi.
Everybody knows if yi laugh at a man in That Way he
will wilt for ever, willn't he?

I was reading this article in a Playboy Magazine
round at my boyfriend's place, or was it Penthouse,   40
anyway, I seem to be spending quite a lot o' time round at
my boyfriend's reading magazines and here it says how
these several top U.S. psychiatrists had done this survey
on how your emotions can sabotage your sexlife even if
you *are* a man and here it blamed the sexually aggressive   45
female of the seventies for the sexual recession of the
eighties. No, apparently it's world wide. Even in Italy
these days women are failing to feel the pinch. The article
says there was a definite swing away from swinging and
back to the values of the fifties. Apparently people are   50
even going back to the fifties contraceptives! Supposed to
be that this whole you know, Ronald Reagan,
Swing-to-the-Right, Fun-Fashion, Fifties thing disny stop
at the glitter-sox the roll-ons and the lurex! It says people
were turning again to the old tried and true spices of   55
Guilt and Feeling Dirty and Furtiveness And Stuff in a
frantic attempt to resurrect the whole sad affair.

My boyfriend says that ladies like me huv been just
too liberated for our own good. Just you mark my words,
he says, the Worm Will Turn.   60

No. 3: Judith.

Men said the small ad in the wants column
am I expecting too much
lady fifty one tall shapely separated
genuine gregarious aware
varied interests vegetarian (own muesli-mix)   65
New Statesman reader romantic sincere
Wishes to share
simple sunshine and undemanding companionship
(view marriage) with
comfortable mature strong nonsmoker sincere   70
adventurous male graduate music-lover (radius
    Hampstead ten miles)
Whole life spent searching for him.
Lady seeks soulmate (or sim.)

No. 4: Kimberley.

Men said the Cosmogirl (eyes
lighting up like dollarsigns in Vegas)   75
Men And How To Hook Them by Tamara Gogetter M.D.
Sip your dulep,◊
slick another coat of Golddigger Red on your fingernails,
Now Read On ...
'A good substitute for a silverspoon is a   80
castiron nerve and wherever the Beautiful People are
Be There –
even if you have to hock your last
Hermes scarf to raise the fare.
(P.S. spas are passé and so is San Trop).   85
Consider Best Bars as a first resort,
regard the single cocktail you'll shell out for as
sheer investment, get yourself
gift wrapped, send for our jetset silklook shirt,
rid yourself of   90
even that inch-of-pinch and the
body beautiful will be guaranteed bait for

ace race driver or millionaire financier in advanced stages
of senility.
(Offer subject to availability.) 95

No. 5: Mo.

Men says My Boss
are definitely more dependable
and though even in these days of equal pay
men tend to come a wee bitty more expensive
due to the added responsibility a man tends to have 100
in his jobspecification
Well for instance you can depend on a man not to get pregnant.
My Boss says men are more objective.
Catch a man bitching
about healthhazards and conditions 105
and going out on strike over no papertowels in the toilet
or nagging over the lack of day nursery facilities
My Boss says as far as he's concerned a crêche is a motor
    accident in Kelvinside°
and any self respecting woman should have a good man
to take care of her so its only pinmoney anyway 110
and that's bound to come out in the attitude.
Well a man isn't subject to moods
or premenstrual tension a guy
isn't going to phone in sick with some crap about cramps.
My Boss says a man rings in 115
with an upset stomach and you know either
he means a hangover or else his brother
managed to get him a ticket for Wembley.

You know where you are with a man.

No. 6: Bette.

Men said the housewife   120
(Waiting for the coffee to perk)
Honestly, Muriel, men!
(Wringing her apron in mock indignation)
That's the third time this week I've picked his
Good polyester-dacron trousers up off the floor and   125
Hung them up in their crease.
What's the use?
Doesn't lift a finger, does David
Never a handsturn from him, believe me.
The kitchenette is a closed book.   130
Don't you be downtrodden Muriel.
Make that clear from the start.

Men, honestly, wee boys at heart.
Men!

Favourite Shade (Rap)

She's getting No More Black, her.
You've got bugger all bar black, Barbra.
Black's dead drab an' all.
Ah'd never have been seen
deid in it, your age tae!   5
Dreich.° As a shade it's draining.
Better aff
somethin tae pit a bit a colour in her cheeks, eh no?

Black. Hale wardrobe fulla black claes.
Jist hingin' therr half the time, emmty.   10
On the hangers, hingin.
Plus by the way a gloryhole
Chockablock with bermuda shorts, the lot.
Yella kimono, ah don't know
whit all.   15
Tropical prints.
Polyester everything Easy-Kerr. Bit naw, naw
that was last year, noo
she's no one to give
nothing coloured   20
houseroom. Black. Black.
Ah'm fed up tae the back teeth lukkin' ett her.
Feyther says the same.

Who's peyin' fur it onlywey?
Wance yir workin' weer whit yi like.   25
No as if yiv nothin' tae pit oan yir back.
Black!
As well oot the world as oot the fashion.

Seen a wee skirt in Miss Selfridge.
Sort of dove, it was lovely.   30
Would she weer it, but?
Goes: see if it was black
If it was black
it'd be brilliant.

Men Talk (Rap)

Women
Rabbit rabbit rabbit women
Tattle and titter
Women prattle
Women waffle and witter   5

Men Talk. Men Talk.

Women into Girl Talk
About Women's Trouble
Trivia 'n' Small Talk
They yap and they babble   10

Men Talk. Men Talk.

Women gossip Women giggle
Women niggle-niggle-niggle
Men Talk.

Women yatter   15
Women chatter
Women chew the fat, women spill the beans
Women aint been takin'
The oh-so Good Advice in them
Women's Magazines.   20

A Man Likes A Good Listener.

Oh yeah
I like A Woman
Who likes me enough
Not to nitpick   25
Not to nag and
Not to interrupt 'cause I call that treason
A woman with the Good Grace
To be struck dumb
By me Sweet Reason. Yes –   30

A Man Likes a Good Listener
A Real
Man
Likes a Real Good Listener

Women yap yap yap   35
Verbal Diarrhoea is a Female Disease
Woman she spread she rumours round she
Like Philadelphia Cream Cheese.

Oh
Bossy Women Gossip   40
Girlish Women Giggle
Women natter, women nag
Women niggle niggle niggle

Men Talk.

Men   45
Think First, Speak Later
Men Talk.

Jackie Kay

✦

In *The Adoption Papers* sequence, the voices of the three speakers are distinguished typographically:

DAUGHTER: Sabon typeface
ADOPTIVE MOTHER: Meta typeface
BIRTH MOTHER: Christiana typeface

The Adoption Papers

I always wanted to give birth
do that incredible natural thing
that women do – I nearly broke down
when I heard we couldn't,
and then my man said   5
well there's always adoption
(we didn't have test tubes and the rest then)
even in the early sixties there was
something scandalous about adopting,
telling the world your secret failure   10
bringing up an alien child,
who knew what it would turn out to be

I was pulled out with forceps
left a gash down my left cheek
four months inside a glass cot   15
but she came faithful
from Glasgow to Edinburgh
and peered through the glass
I must have felt somebody willing me to survive;
she would not pick another baby   20

I still have the baby photograph
I keep it in my bottom drawer

She is twenty-six today
my hair is grey

The skin around my neck is wrinkling   25
does she imagine me this way

Part One: 1961–1962

Chapter 1: The Seed

I never thought it would be quicker
than walking down the mainstreet

I want to stand in front of the mirror
swollen bellied so swollen bellied   30

The time, the exact time
for that particular seed to be singled out

I want to lie on my back at night
I want to pee all the time

amongst all others   35
like choosing a dancing partner

I crave discomfort like some women
crave chocolate or earth or liver

Now these slow weeks on
I can't stop going over and over   40

I can't believe I've tried for five years
for something that could take five minutes

It only took a split second
not a minute or more.

I want the pain   45
the tearing searing pain

I want my waters to break
like Noah's flood

I want to push and push
and scream and scream.   50

When I was sure I wrote a short note
six weeks later – a short letter

He was sorry; we should have known better
He couldn't leave Nigeria.

I missed him, silly things   55
his sudden high laugh,

His eyes intense as whirlwind
the music he played me

Chapter 2: The Original Birth Certificate

I say to the man at the desk
I'd like my original birth certificate   60
Do you have any idea what your name was?
Close, close he laughs. *Well what was it?*

So slow as torture he discloses bit by bit
my mother's name, my original name
the hospital I was born in, the time I came.   65

Outside Edinburgh is soaked in sunshine
I talk to myself walking past the castle.
So, so, so, I was a midnight baby after all.

I am nineteen
my whole life is changing 70

On the first night
I see her shuttered eyes in my dreams

I cannot pretend she's never been
my stitches pull and threaten to snap

my own body a witness 75
leaking blood to sheets, milk to shirts

On the second night
I'll suffocate her with a feather pillow

Bury her under a weeping willow
Or take her far out to sea 80

and watch her tiny eight-pound body
sink to shells and reshape herself.

So much the better than her body
encased in glass like a museum piece

On the third night 85
I toss I did not go through these months

for you to die on me now
on the third night I lie

willing life into her
breathing air all the way down the corridor 90

to the glass cot
I push my nipples through

Chapter 3: The Waiting Lists

The first agency we went to
didn't want us on their lists,
we didn't live close enough to a church   95
nor were we church-goers
(though we kept quiet about being communists).
The second told us
we weren't high enough earners.
The third liked us   100
but they had a five-year waiting list.
I spent six months trying not to look
at swings nor the front of supermarket trolleys,
not to think this kid I've wanted could be five.
The fourth agency was full up.   105
The fifth said yes but again no babies.
Just as we were going out the door
I said oh you know we don't mind the colour.
Just like that, the waiting was over.

This morning a slim manilla envelope arrives   110
postmarked Edinburgh: one piece of paper
I have now been able to look up your microfiche
(as this is all the records kept nowadays).
From your mother's letters, the following information:
Your mother was nineteen when she had you.   115
You weighed eight pounds four ounces.
She liked hockey. She worked in Aberdeen
as a waitress. She was five foot eight inches.

I thought I'd hid everything
that there wasnie wan   120
giveaway sign left

I put Marx Engels Lenin (no Trotsky)
in the airing cupboard – she'll no be
checking out the towels surely

39

All the copies of the *Daily Worker*   125
I shoved under the sofa
the dove of peace I took down from the loo

A poster of Paul Robeson[◇]
saying give him his passport
I took down from the kitchen   130

I left a bust of Burns[◇]
my detective stories
and the Complete Works of Shelley[◇]

She comes at 11.30 exactly.
I pour her coffee   135
from my new Hungarian set

And foolishly pray she willnae
ask its origins – honestly
this baby is going to my head.

She crosses her legs on the sofa   140
I fancy I hear the *Daily Workers*
rustle underneath her

Well she says, you have an interesting home
She sees my eyebrows rise.
It's different she qualifies.   145

Hell and I've spent all morning
trying to look ordinary
– a lovely home for the baby.

She buttons her coat all smiles
I'm thinking   150
I'm on the home run

But just as we get to the last post
her eye catches at the same times as mine
a red ribbon with twenty world peace badges

Clear as a hammer and sickle   155
on the wall.
Oh, she says are you against nuclear weapons?

To Hell with this. Baby or no baby.
Yes I says. Yes yes yes.
I'd like this baby to live in a nuclear free world.   160

Oh. Her eyes light up.
I'm all for peace myself she says,
and sits down for another cup of coffee.

Chapter 4: Baby Lazarus◇

Land moves like driven cattle
My eyes snatch pieces of news   165
headlines strung out on a line:
MOTHER DROWNS BABY IN THE CLYDE

November

The social worker phoned,
our baby is a girl but not healthy   170
she won't pass the doctor's test
until she's well. The adoption papers
can't be signed. I put the phone down.
I felt all hot. Don't get overwrought.
What does she expect? I'm not a mother   175
until I've signed that piece of paper.

The rhythm of the train carries me
over the frigid earth
the constant chug a comforter
a rocking cradle.   180

Maybe the words lie
across my forehead
headline in thin ink
MOTHER GIVES BABY AWAY

December   185

We drove through to Edinburgh,
I was that excited the forty miles
seemed a lifetime. What do you think she'll
look like? I don't know my man says. I could tell
he was as nervous as me. On the way back his face   190
was one long smile even although
he didn't get inside. Only me.
I wore a mask but she didn't seem to mind
I told her *any day now my darling any day.*

Nobody would ever guess.   195
I had no other choice
Anyway it's best for her,
My name signed on a dotted line.

March

Our baby has passed.   200
We can pick her up in two days.
Two days for Christ's sake,
could they not have given us a bit more notice?

Land moves like driven cattle

I must stop it. Put it out my mind.   205
There is no use going over and over.
I'm glad she's got a home to go to.
This sandwich is plastic.

I forgot to put sugar in the flask.

The man across the table keeps staring.   210
I should have brought another book –
all this character does is kiss and say sorry

go and come back,
we are all foolish with trust.
I used to like winter   215
the empty spaces, the fresh air.

When I got home
I went out into the garden –
the frost bit my old brown boots –
and dug a hole the size of my baby   220
and buried the clothes I'd bought anyway.
A week later I stood at my window
and saw the ground move and swell
the promise of a crop,
that's when she started crying.   225
I gave her a service then, sang
Ye banks and braes, planted
a bush of roses, read the Book of Job,°
cursed myself digging a pit for my baby
sprinkling ash from the grate.   230
Late that same night
she came in by the window,
my baby Lazarus
and suckled at my breast.

Chapter 5: The Tweed Hat Dream

Today I ring the counselling agency in Edinburgh.   235
Can you start to trace through marriage certificates?
It will take three weeks what do you expect from it.
If she wants to meet me that's fine if she doesn't
that is also fine

This morning the counselling woman rings   240
she's found someone who might be her
she's not sure; do I know my grandmother's name?
Pity. She'll be in touch, not sure when.

Her mother just turns up at the door
with a tweed hat on. I thinks   245
she doesn't suit tweed, she's too young.
In all these months I've never put a face to her
that looks like my daughter – so picture me
when I see those lips. She looks a dead spit
except of course she's white; lightning white.   250
She says in her soft Highland voice
can you let me see her? Can you?
What could I do? She comes in swift
as wind in a storm, rushes up the stairs
as if she knows the house already,   255
picks up my baby and strokes her cheeks endlessly
till I get tired and say, I'll be downstairs.

I put the kettle on, maybe
hot tea will redden those white cheeks,
arrange a plate of biscuits which keep   260
sliding onto the floor.
She's been up there helluva long.
I don't know where the thought comes from
but suddenly I'm pounding the stairs
like thunder. Her tweed hat   265
is in the cot. That is all.

That night I turn it through till dawn
a few genes, blood, a birth.
All this bother, certificates, papers.
It is all so long ago. Does it matter?   270
Now I come from her,
the mother who stole my milk teeth
ate the digestive left for Santa

Part Two: 1967–1971

Chapter 6: The Telling Part

Ma mammy bot me oot a shop
Ma mammy says I was a luvly baby 275

Ma mammy picked me (I wiz the best)
your mammy had to take you (she'd no choice)

Ma mammy says she's no really ma mammy
(just kid on)

It's a bit like a part you've rehearsed so well 280
you can't play it on the opening night
She says my real mammy is away far away
Mammy why aren't you and me the same colour
But I love my mammy whether she's real or no
My heart started rat tat tat like a tin drum 285
all the words took off to another planet
Why

But I love ma mammy whether she's real or no

I could hear the upset in her voice
I says *I'm not your real mother,* 290
though Christ knows why I said that,
If I'm not who is, but all my planned speech
went out the window

She took me when I'd nowhere to go

my mammy is the best mammy in the world OK.   295

After mammy telt me she wisnae my real mammy
I was scared to death she was gonnie melt
or something or mibbe disappear in the dead
of night and somebody would say she wis a fairy
godmother. So the next morning I felt her skin   300
to check it was flesh, but mibbe it was just
a good imitation. How could I tell if my mammy
was a dummy with a voice spoken by someone else?
So I searches the whole house for clues
but I never found nothing. Anyhow a day after   305
I got my guinea pig and forgot all about it.

I always believed in the telling anyhow.
You can't keep something like that secret
I wanted her to think of her other mother
out there, thinking that child I had will be   310
seven today eight today all the way up to
god knows when. I told my daughter –
I bet your mother's never missed your birthday,
how could she?

Mammy's face is cherries.   315
She is stirring the big pot of mutton soup
singing *I gave my love a cherry*
it had no stone.
I am up to her apron.
I jump onto her feet and grab her legs   320
like a huge pair of trousers,
she walks round the kitchen lifting me up.

Suddenly I fall off her feet.
And mammy falls to the floor.
She won't stop the song   325
I gave my love a chicken it had no bone.
I run next door for help.
When me and Uncle Alec come back

Mammy's skin is toffee stuck to the floor.
And her bones are all scattered like toys.   330

Now when people say 'ah but
it's not like having your own child though is it',
I say of course it is, what else is it?
she's my child, I have told her stories
wept at her losses, laughed at her pleasures,   335
she is mine.

I was always the first to hear her in the night
all this umbilical knot business is nonsense
– the men can afford deeper sleeps that's all.
I listened to hear her talk,   340
and when she did I heard my voice under hers
and now some of her mannerisms crack me up

Me and my best pal
don't have Donny Osmond° or David Cassidy°
on our walls and we don't wear Starsky and Hutch°   345
jumpers either. Round at her house we put on
the old record player and mime to Pearl Bailey°
Tired of the life I lead, tired of the blues I breed
and Bessie Smith° I can't do without my kitchen man.
Then we practise ballroom dancing giggling,   350
everyone thinks we're dead old-fashioned.

Chapter 7: Black Bottom°

Maybe that's why I don't like
all this talk about her being black,
I brought her up as my own
as I would any other child   355
colour matters to the nutters;
but she says my daughter says
it matters to her

47

I suppose there would have been things
I couldn't understand with any child,   360
we knew she was coloured.
They told us they had no babies at first
and I chanced it didn't matter what colour it was
and they said *oh well are you sure*
in that case we have a baby for you –   365
to think she wasn't even thought of as a baby,
my baby, my baby

I chase his *Sambo Sambo* all the way from the school gate.
A fistful of anorak – What did you call me? Say that again.
Sam-bo. He plays the word like a bouncing ball   370
but his eyes move fast as ping pong.
I shove him up against the wall,
say that again you wee shite. *Sambo, sambo*, he's crying now

I knee him in the balls. What was that?
My fist is steel; I punch and punch his gut.   375
Sorry I didn't hear you? His tears drip like wax.
Nothing he heaves *I didn't say nothing*.
I let him go. He is a rat running. He turns
and shouts *Dirty Darkie* I chase him again.
Blonde hairs in my hand. Excuse me!   380
This teacher from primary 7 stops us.
Names? I'll report you to the headmaster tomorrow.
But Miss. Save it for Mr Thompson she says

My teacher's face cracks into a thin smile
Her long nails scratch the note well well   385
I see you were fighting yesterday, again.
In a few years time you'll be a juvenile delinquent.
Do you know what that is? Look it up in the dictionary.
She spells each letter with slow pleasure.
Read it out to the class.   390
Thug. Vandal. Hooligan. Speak up. Have you lost your tongue?

To be honest I hardly ever think about it
except if something happens, you know
daft talk about darkies. Racialism.
Mothers ringing my bell with their kids   395
crying *You tell. You tell. You tell.*
– *No.* You tell your little girl to stop calling
my little girl names and I'll tell my little girl
to stop giving your little girl a doing.

We're practising for the school show   400
I'm trying to do the Cha Cha and the Black Bottom
but I can't get the steps right
my right foot's left and my left foot's right
my teacher shouts from the bottom
of the class Come on, show   405

us what you can do I thought
you people had it in your blood.
My skin is hot as burning coal
like that time she said Darkies are like coal
in front of the whole class – my blood   410
what does she mean? I thought

she'd stopped all that after the last time
my dad talked to her on parents' night
the other kids are all right till she starts;
my feet step out of time, my heart starts   415
to miss beats like when I can't sleep at night –
What Is In My Blood? The bell rings, it is time.

Sometimes it is hard to know what to say
that will comfort. Us two in the armchair;
me holding her breath, 'they're ignorant   420
let's have some tea and cake, forget them'.

Maybe it's really Bette Davis I
want to be the good twin or even better the bad
one or a nanny who drowns a baby in a bath.

I'm not sure maybe I'd prefer Katharine   425
Hepburn tossing my red hair, having a hot
temper. I says to my teacher Can't I be
Elizabeth Taylor, drunk and fat and she
just laughed, not much chance of that.
I went for an audition for *The Prime*   430
of Miss Jean Brodie.◇ I didn't get a part
even though I've been acting longer
than Beverley Innes. So I have. Honest.

Olubayo was the colour of peat
when we walked out heads turned   435
like horses, folk stood like trees
their eyes fixed on us – it made me
burn, that hot glare; my hand
would sweat down to his bone.
Finally, alone, we'd melt   440
nothing, nothing would matter

He never saw her. I looked for him in her;
for a second it was as if he was there
in that glass cot looking back through her.

On my bedroom wall is a big poster   445
of Angela Davis◇ who is in prison
right now for nothing at all
except she wouldn't put up with stuff.
My mum says she is *only* 26
which seems really old to me   450
but my mum says it is young

just imagine, she says, being on
America's Ten Most Wanted People's List at 26!
I can't.
Angela Davis is the only female person   455
I've seen (except for a nurse on TV)
who looks like me. She had big hair like mine
that grows out instead of down.

My mum says it's called an *Afro*.
If I could be as brave as her when I get older   460
I'll be OK.
Last night I kissed her goodnight again
and wondered if she could feel the kisses
in prison all the way from Scotland.
Her skin is the same too you know.   465
I can see my skin is that colour
but most of the time I forget,
so sometimes when I look in the mirror
I give myself a bit of a shock
and say to myself *Do you really look like this?*   470
as if I'm somebody else. I wonder if she does that.

I don't believe she killed anybody.
It is all a load of phoney lies.
My dad says it's a set up.
I asked him if she'll get the electric chair   475
like them Roseberries° he was telling me about.
No he says the world is on her side.
Well how come she's in there then I thinks.
I worry she's going to get the chair.
I worry she's worrying about the chair.   480
My dad says she'll be putting on a brave face.
He brought me a badge home which I wore
to school. It says FREE ANGELA DAVIS.
And all my pals says 'Who's she?'

Part Three: 1980–1990

Chapter 8: Generations

The sun went out just like that   485
almost as if it had never been,
hard to imagine now the way it fell
on treetops, thatched roofs, people's faces.
Suddenly the trees lost their nerves
and the grass passed the wind on   490
blade to blade, fast as gossip

Years later, the voices still come close
especially in dreams, not distant echoes
loud – a pneumatic drill – deeper and deeper still.
I lived the scandal, wore it casual   495
as a summer's dress, Jesus sandals.
All but the softest whisper:
she's lost an awful lot of weight.

Now my secret is the hush of heavy curtains drawn.
I dread strange handwriting   500
sometimes jump when the phone rings,
she is all of nineteen and legally able.
At night I lie practising my lines
but 'sorry' never seems large enough
nor 'I can't see you, yes, I'll send a photograph.'   505

I was pulled out with forceps
left a gash down my left cheek
four months inside a glass cot

but
she came faithful from Glasgow to Edinburgh 510
and peered through the glass
she would not pick another baby.

I don't know what diseases
come down my line;
when dentist and doctors ask 515
the old blood questions about family runnings
I tell them: I have no nose or mouth or eyes
to match, no spitting image or dead cert,
my face watches itself in the glass.

I have my parents who are not of the same tree 520
and you keep trying to make it matter,
the blood, the tie, the passing down
generations.
We all have our contradictions,
the ones with the mother's nose and father's eyes 525
have them;
the blood does not bind confusion,
yet I confess to my contradiction
I want to know my blood.

I know my blood. 530
It is dark ruby red and comes
regular and I use Lillets.
I know my blood when I cut my finger.
I know what my blood looks like.

It is the well, the womb, the fucking seed. 535
Here, I am far enough away to wonder –
what were their faces like
who were my grandmothers
what were the days like
passed in Scotland 540
the land I come from
the soil in my blood.

Put it this way:
I know she thinks of me often
when the light shows its face   545
or the dark skulks behind hills,
she conjures me up or I just appear
when I take the notion, my slippers
are silent and I walk through doors.

She's lying in bed; I wake her up   550
a pinch on her cheek is enough,
then I make her think of me for hours.
The best thing I can steal is sleep.
I get right under the duvet and murmur
you'll never really know your mother.   555
I know who she thinks I am – she's made a blunder.

She is faceless
She has no nose
She is five foot eight inches tall
She likes hockey best   560
She is twenty-six today
She was a waitress
My hair is grey
She wears no particular dress
The skin around my neck is wrinkling   565
Does she imagine me this way?
Lately I make pictures of her
But I can see the smallness
She is tall and slim
of her hands, Yes   570
Her hair is loose curls
an opal stone on her middle finger
I reach out to catch her
Does she talk broad Glasgow?
But no matter how fast   575
Maybe they moved years ago
I run after

She is faceless, she never
weeps. She has neither eyes nor
fine boned cheeks   580

Once would be enough,
just to listen to her voice
watch the way she moves her hands
when she talks.

Chapter 9: The Phone Call

I have had my grandmother's Highland number   585
for four months now burning a hole in my filofax.

Something this morning gives me courage
to close the kitchen door and dial.

My grandmother's voice sounds much younger
'I used to work ages ago with your daughter   590

Elizabeth, do you have her present address?'
Sorry, she says, *No, but one of the girls*

will have it. She gives me another Highland number
wishing me luck. *What did you say your name was?*

Thirty minutes later my mother's sister   595
asks lots of questions – *Where did you work?*

How long ago was that? What age are you?
Forty I lie. *For a minute I thought ...*   600

But if you're forty, you can't be.
I know she knows. The game's a bogey.

Actually I'm 26. *I thought so love.*
I thought it was you. Mam knew too.

She just rang to warn me you'd ring.
How are you? How's your life been?

I'll give her yours. She'll write. 605
I'm sure you understand. I do. I do.

Now she's gone. I get phone calls regularly.
It's not that I think I'm losing out but
I've surprised myself just the same;
I've had to stop myself saying, 'drop 610
it, you'll get hurt'. I do worry
of course I do, but it's me that's hurt.
Tonight I cried watching bloody Adam
Carrington° discover he's not a Carrington
any more. Daft. Getting myself into a tizzy. 615

Chapter 10: The Meeting Dream

If I picture it like this it hurts less
We are both shy
though our eyes are not,
they pierce below skin.
We are not as we imagined: 620
I am smaller, fatter, darker
I am taller, thinner
and I'd always imagined her hair dark brown
not grey. I can see my chin in hers
that is all, though no doubt 625
my mum will say, when she looks at the photo,
she's your double she really is.

There is no sentiment in this living-room,
a plain wood table and a few books.
We don't cuddle or even shake hands   630
though we smile sudden as a fire blazing
then die down.
Her hands play with her wedding-ring,
I've started smoking again.

We don't ask big questions even later by the shore.   635
We walk slow, tentative as crabs
No, so what have you been doing the past 26 years.
Just what are you working at, stuff like that.

Ages later I pick up a speckled stone
and hurl it into the sea,   640
is this how you imagined it to be?
I never imagined it.
Oh. I hear the muffled splash.
It would have driven me mad imagining,
26 years is a long time.   645

Inside once more I sip hot tea
notice one wood-framed photo.
The air is as old as the sea.
I stare at her chin till she makes me look down.
Her hands are awkward as rocks.   650
My eyes are stones washed over and over.

If I picture it like this it hurts less

One dream cuts another open like a gutted fish
nothing is what it was;
she is too many imaginings to be flesh and blood.   655
There is nothing left to say.
Neither of us mentions meeting again.

When I'm by myself watching the box
it's surprising how often it crops

up; that he or she didn't know anything about it 660
and now who is he or she really
do they love who they thought they loved
et cetera. You've got the picture.
Mine knew. As soon as possible
I always told her, if you ever want to, 665
I won't mind. I wasn't trying to be big
about it – if that was me, that's how I'd be.
Curiosity. It's natural. Origins.
That kind of thing. See me and her
there is no mother and daughter more similar. 670
We're on the wavelength so we are.
Right away I know if she's upset.
And vice versa. Closer than blood.
Thicker than water. Me and my daughter.

I wrapped up well and went out before 675
The birds began their ritual blether◊

I wrapped her up in purple wrapping paper
And threw her down the old well near here.
There was no sound, it's no longer
In use – years – she's been in my drawer 680
Faded now, she's not a baby any more

Still pitch dark. It didn't matter.
I know every bend. I've no more terror.
Going home, the light spilled like water.

Her sister said she'd write me a letter. 685
In the morning I'm awake with the birds
waiting for the crash of the letter box
then the soft thud of words on the matt.
I lie there, duvet round my shoulders
fantasising the colour of her paper 690
whether she'll underline First Class
or have a large circle over her 'i's.

Carol Ann Duffy

Comprehensive

Tutumantu is like hopscotch, Kwani-kwani is like
   hide-and-seek.
When my sister came back to Africa she could only speak
English. Sometimes we fought in bed because she didn't know
what I was saying. I like Africa better than England.
My mother says You will like it when we get our own house.   5
We talk a lot about the things we used to do
in Africa and then we are happy.

Wayne. Fourteen. Games are for kids. I support
the National Front. Paki-bashing and pulling girls'
knickers down. Dad's got his own mini-cab. We watch   10
the video. I Spit on Your Grave. Brilliant.
I don't suppose I'll get a job. It's all them
coming over here to work. Arsenal.

Masjid◇ at 6 o'clock. School at 8. There was
a friendly shop selling rice. They ground it at home   15
to make the evening nan. Families face Mecca.
There was much more room to play than here in London.
We played in an old village. It is empty now.
We got a plane to Heathrow. People wrote to us
that everything was easy here.   20

It's boring. Get engaged. Probably work in Safeways
worst luck. I haven't lost it yet because I want
respect. Marlon Frederic's nice but he's a bit dark.
I like Madness. The lead singer's dead good.
My mum is bad with her nerves. She won't   25
let me do nothing. Michelle. It's just boring.

Ejaz.* They put some sausages on my plate.
As I was going to put one in my mouth
a Moslem boy jumped on me and pulled.
The plate dropped on the floor and broke. He asked me
    in Urdu   30
if I was a Moslem. I said Yes. You shouldn't be eating this.
It's a pig's meat. So we became friends.

My sister went out with one. There was murder.
I'd like to be mates, but they're different from us.
Some of them wear turbans in class. You can't help   35
taking the piss. I'm going in the Army.
No choice really. When I get married
I might emigrate. A girl who can cook
with long legs. Australia sounds all right.

Some of my family are named after the Moghul emperors. 40
Aurangzeb, Jehangir, Batur, Humayun. I was born
thirteen years ago in Jhelum. This is a hard school.
A man came in with a milk crate. The teacher told us
to drink our milk. I didn't understand what she was saying,
so I didn't go to get any milk. I have hope and am ambitious. 45
At first I felt as if I was dreaming, but I wasn't.
Everything I saw was true.

Head of English

Today we have a poet in the class.
A real live poet with a published book.
Notice the inkstained fingers girls. Perhaps
we're going to witness verse hot from the press.
Who knows. Please show your appreciation   5
by clapping. Not too loud. Now

sit up straight and listen. Remember
the lesson on assonance, for not all poems,
sadly, rhyme these days. Still. Never mind.
Whispering's, as always, out of bounds –   10
but do feel free to raise some questions.
After all, we're paying forty pounds.

Those of you with English Second Language
see me after break. We're fortunate
to have this person in our midst.   15
Season of mists and so on and so forth.
I've written quite a bit of poetry myself,
am doing Kipling with the Lower Fourth.

Right. That's enough from me. On with the Muse.
Open a window at the back. We don't   20
want winds of change about the place.
Take notes, but don't write reams. Just an essay
on the poet's themes. Fine. Off we go.
Convince us that there's something we don't know.

Well. Really. Run along now girls. I'm sure   25
that gave an insight to an outside view.
Applause will do. Thank you
very much for coming here today. Lunch
in the hall? Do hang about. Unfortunately
I have to dash. Tracey will show you out.   30

Education for Leisure

Today I am going to kill something. Anything.
I have had enough of being ignored and today
I am going to play God. It is an ordinary day,
a sort of grey with boredom stirring in the streets.

I squash a fly against the window with my thumb.   5
We did that at school. Shakespeare. It was in
another language and now the fly is in another language.
I breathe out talent on the glass to write my name.

I am a genius. I could be anything at all, with half
the chance. But today I am going to change the world.   10
Something's world. The cat avoids me. The cat
knows I am a genius and has hidden itself.

I pour the goldfish down the bog. I pull the chain.
I see that it is good. The budgie is panicking.
Once a fortnight, I walk the two miles into town   15
for signing on. They don't appreciate my autograph.

There is nothing left to kill. I dial the radio
and tell the man he's talking to a superstar.
He cuts me off. I get our bread-knife and go out.
The pavements glitter suddenly. I touch your arm.   20

Debt

He was all night sleepless over money.
Impossible scenarios danced in the dark
as though he was drunk. The woman
stirred, a soft spoon, and what had emerged
from them dreamed in the next room, safe.   5
He left himself and drew a gun he didn't own.

He won the pools; pearls for her and ponies
for the kids. The damp bedroom was an ocean-liner
till the woman farted, drifted on, away from him.
Despair formed a useless prayer and worry an ulcer.   10
He bargained with something he could not believe in
for something he could not have. *Sir...*

Through the wallpaper men in suits appeared.
They wanted the video, wanted the furniture.
They wanted the children. Sweat soured in nylon sheets   15
as his heartbeat panicked, trying to get out.
There was nothing he would not do. There was
nothing to do but run the mind's mad films.

Dear Sir ... his ghost typed on. He remembered
waiting for her, years ago, on pay-day   20
with a bar of fruit-and-nut. Somehow consoled
he reached out, found her, and then slept.
Add this. Take that away. The long night leaked
cold light into the house. A letter came.

Standing Female Nude

Six hours like this for a few francs.
Belly nipple arse in the window light,
he drains the colour from me. Further to the right,
Madame. And do try to be still.
I shall be represented analytically and hung   5
in great museums. The bourgeoisie will coo
at such an image of a river-whore. They call it Art.

Maybe. He is concerned with volume, space.
I with the next meal. You're getting thin,
Madame, this is not good. My breasts hang   10
slightly low, the studio is cold. In the tea-leaves
I can see the Queen of England gazing
on my shape. Magnificent, she murmurs
moving on. It makes me laugh. His name

is Georges. They tell me he's a genius.   15
There are times he does not concentrate
and stiffens for my warmth. Men think of their mothers.
He possesses me on canvas as he dips the brush
repeatedly into the paint. Little man,
you've not the money for the arts I sell.   20
Both poor, we make our living how we can.

I ask him Why do you do this? Because
I have to. There's no choice. Don't talk.
My smile confuses him. These artists
take themselves too seriously. At night I fill myself   25
with wine and dance around the bars. When it's finished
he shows me proudly, lights a cigarette. I say
Twelve francs and get my shawl. It does not look like me.

War Photographer

In his darkroom he is finally alone
with spools of suffering set out in ordered rows.
The only light is red and softly glows,
as though this were a church and he
a priest preparing to intone a Mass.   5
Belfast. Beirut. Phnom Penh.° All flesh is grass.

He has a job to do. Solutions slop in trays
beneath his hands which did not tremble then
though seem to now. Rural England. Home again
to ordinary pain which simple weather can dispel,   10
to fields which don't explode beneath the feet
of running children in a nightmare heat.

Something is happening. A stranger's features
faintly start to twist before his eyes,
a half-formed ghost. He remembers the cries   15
of this man's wife, how he sought approval
without words to do what someone must
and how the blood stained into foreign dust.

A hundred agonies in black-and-white
from which his editor will pick out five or six   20
for Sunday's supplement. The reader's eyeballs prick
with tears between the bath and pre-lunch beers.
From the aeroplane he stares impassively at where
he earns his living and they do not care.

Originally

We came from our own country in a red room
which fell through the fields, our mother singing
our father's name to the turn of the wheels.
My brothers cried, one of them bawling *Home,*
Home, as the miles rushed back to the city,   5
the street, the house, the vacant rooms
where we didn't live any more. I stared
at the eyes of a blind toy, holding its paw.

All childhood is an emigration. Some are slow,
leaving you standing, resigned, up an avenue   10
where no one you know stays. Others are sudden.
Your accent wrong. Corners, which seem familiar,
leading to unimagined, pebble-dashed estates, big boys
eating worms and shouting words you don't understand.
My parents' anxiety stirred like a loose tooth   15
in my head. *I want our own country*, I said.

But then you forget, or don't recall, or change,
and, seeing your brother swallow a slug, feel only
a skelf of shame. I remember my tongue
shedding its skin like a snake, my voice   20
in the classroom sounding just like the rest. Do I only think
I lost a river, culture, speech, sense of first space
and the right place? Now, *Where do you come from?*
strangers ask. *Originally?* And I hesitate.

In Mrs Tilscher's Class

You could travel up the Blue Nile
with your finger, tracing the route
while Mrs Tilscher chanted the scenery.
Tana. Ethiopia. Khartoum. Aswân.
That for an hour, then a skittle of milk   5
and the chalky Pyramids rubbed into dust.
A window opened with a long pole.
The laugh of a bell swung by a running child.

This was better than home. Enthralling books.
The classroom glowed like a sweet shop.   10
Sugar paper. Coloured shapes. Brady and Hindley◇
faded, like the faint, uneasy smudge of a mistake.
Mrs Tilscher loved you. Some mornings, you found
she'd left a good gold star by your name.
The scent of a pencil slowly, carefully, shaved.   15
A xylophone's nonsense heard from another form.

Over the Easter term, the inky tadpoles changed
from commas into exclamation marks. Three frogs
hopped in the playground, freed by a dunce,
followed by a line of kids, jumping and croaking   20
away from the lunch queue. A rough boy
told you how you were born. You kicked him, but stared
at your parents, appalled, when you got back home.

That feverish July, the air tasted of electricity.
A tangible alarm made you always untidy, hot,   25
fractious under the heavy, sexy sky. You asked her
how you were born and Mrs Tilscher smiled,
then turned away. Reports were handed out.
You ran through the gates, impatient to be grown,
as the sky split open into a thunderstorm.   30

The Literature Act

My poem will be a fantasy about living in a high-rise flat,
on the edge of a dirty industrial town, as the lawful wife
    of a yob
who spent the morning demonstrating in the market square
for the benefit of the gutter press. This was against a book
of which he violently disapproves and which was written
    by some cunt   5
who is a blasphemer or a lesbian or whose filth is being studied
in our local schools as part of some pisspot exam, the bastard.
I feel a thrill of fear as I imagine frying his evening meal
and keeping his children quiet as he shouts at the News. Later
he will thrash in the bed, like a fish out of water, not censoring   10
the words and pictures in his head. I would like my poem
to be given to such a man by the Police. Should he resist
I would like him to be taken to court; where the Jury,
the Judge, will compel him to learn it by heart. Every word.

Translating the English, 1989

' ... and much of the poetry, alas, is lost in translation ... '

Welcome to my country! We have here Edwina Currie
and The Sun newspaper. Much excitement.
Also the weather has been most improving
even in February. Daffodils. (Wordsworth. Up North.) If
    you like
Shakespeare or even Opera we have too the Black Market.   5
For two hundred quids we are talking Les Miserables,
nods being as good as winks. Don't eat the eggs.
Wheel-clamp. Dogs. Vagrants. A tour of our wonderful
capital city is not to be missed. The Fergie,
The Princess Di and the football hooligan, truly you will   10
like it here, Squire. Also we can be talking crack, smack
and Carling Black Label if we are so inclined. Don't
drink the H_2O. All very proud we now have
a green Prime Minister. What colour yours? Binbags.
You will be knowing of Charles Dickens and Terry Wogan   15
and Scotland. All this can be arranged for cash no questions.
Ireland not on. Fish and chips and the Official Secrets Act
second to none. Here we go. We are liking
a smashing good time like estate agents and Neighbours,
also Brookside for we are allowed four Channels.   20
How many you have? Last night of Proms. Andrew
Lloyd-Webber. Jeffrey Archer. Plenty culture you will be
    agreeing.
Also history and buildings. The Houses of Lords. Docklands.
Many thrills and high interest rates for own good. Muggers.
Much lead in petrol. Filth. Rule Britannia and child abuse.   25
Electronic tagging, Boss, ten pints and plenty rape. Queen
    Mum.
Channel Tunnel. You get here fast no problem to my country
my country my country welcome welcome welcome.

Too Bad

It was winter. Wilson had just said
we should have one in The Dog. So we did,
running through the blue wet streets
with our heads down, laughing, to get there,
down doubles in front of our drenched reflections.   5
The barmaid caught my eye in the mirror. Beautiful.

We had a job to do, but not till closing-time,
hard men knocking back the brandy, each of us
wearing revenge like a badge on his heart. Hatred
dresses in cheap anonymous suits, the kind   10
with an inside pocket for a small gun. *Good Health.*
I smiled at her. Warm rain, like blood, ran down my back.

I remembered my first time, my trembling hand
and Big Frank Connell hissing *Get a grip.*
Tonight, professional, I walked with the boys   15
along a filthy alley to the other pub, the one
where it happened, the one where the man
was putting on his coat, ready for home.

Home. Two weeks in a safe house and I'd be there,
glad of familiar accents and my dull wife.   20
He came out of a side door, clutching a carry-out.
Simple. Afterwards, Wilson was singing *dada da da
Tom Someone, hang down your head and cry.*
Too bad. I fancied that barmaid all right.

Poet for Our Times

I write the headlines for a Daily Paper.
It's just a knack one's born with all-right-Squire.
You do not have to be an educator,
just bang the words down like they're screaming *Fire!*
CECIL-KEAYS ROW SHOCK TELLS EYETIE WAITER.   5
ENGLAND FAN CALLS WHINGEING FROG A LIAR.

Cheers. Thing is, you've got to grab attention
with just one phrase as punters rush on by.
I've made mistakes too numerous to mention,
so now we print the buggers inches high.   10
TOP MP PANTIE ROMP INCREASES TENSION.
RENT BOY: ROCK STAR PAID ME WELL TO LIE.

I like to think that I'm a sort of poet
for our times. My shout. Know what I mean?
I've got a special talent and I show it   15
in punchy haikus featuring the Queen.
DIPLOMAT IN BED WITH SERBO-CROAT.
EASTENDERS' BONKING SHOCK IS WELL-OBSCENE.

Of course, these days, there's not the sense of panic
you got a few years back. What with the box   20
et cet. I wish I'd been around when the Titanic
sank. To headline that, mate, would've been the tops.
SEE PAGE 3 TODAY GENTS THEY'RE GIGANTIC.
KINNOCK-BASHER MAGGIE PULLS OUT STOPS.

And, yes, I have a dream – make that a scotch, ta –   25
that kids will know my headlines off by heart.
IMMIGRANTS FLOOD IN CLAIMS HEATHROW WATCHER.
GREEN PARTY WOMAN IS A NIGHTCLUB TART.
The poems of the decade ... *Stuff 'em! Gotcha!*
The instant tits and bottom line of art.   30

Job Creation

for Ian McMillan

They have shipped Gulliver up north.
He lies at the edge of the town,
sleeping.
His snores are thunder in the night.

Round here, we reckon they have drugged him   5
or we dream he is a landscape
which might drag itself up and walk.

Here are ropes, they said.
Tie him down.
We will pay you.   10
Tie Gulliver down with these ropes.

I slaved all day at his left knee,
until the sun went down
behind it
and clouds gathered on his eyes   15

and darkness settled on his shoulders
like a job.

Making Money

Turnover. Profit. Readies. Cash. Loot. Dough. Income. Stash.
Dosh. Bread. Finance. Brass. I give my tongue over
to money; the taste of warm rust in a chipped mug
of tap-water. Drink some yourself. Consider
an Indian man in Delhi, Salaamat the *niyariwallah*,°   5
who squats by an open drain for hours, sifting shit
for the price of a chapati. More than that. His hands
in crumbling gloves of crap pray at the drains
for the pearls in slime his grandfather swore he found.

Megabucks. Wages. Interest. Wealth. I sniff and snuffle   10
for a whiff of pelf; the stench of an abattoir blown
by a stale wind over the fields. Roll up a fiver,
snort. Meet Kim. Kim will give you the works,
her own worst enema, suck you, lick you, squeal
red weals to your whip, be nun, nurse, nanny,   15
nymph on a credit card. Don't worry.
Kim's only in it for the money. Lucre. Tin. Dibs.

I put my ear to brass lips; a small fire's whisper
close to a forest. Listen. His cellular telephone
rings in the Bull's car. Golden hello. Big deal. Now get this 20
straight. *Making a living is making a killing these days.*
Jobbers and brokers buzz. He paints out a landscape
by number. The Bull. Seriously rich. Nasty. One of us.

Salary. Boodle. Oof. Blunt. Shekels. Lolly. Gelt. Funds.
I wallow in coin, naked; the scary caress of a fake hand   25
on my flesh. Get stuck in. Bergama.° The boys from the
    bazaar
hide on the target-range, watching the soldiers fire.
    Between bursts,

they rush for the spent shells, cart them away for scrap.
Here is the catch. Some shells don't explode. Ahmat
runs over grass, lucky for six months, so far. So   30
bomb-collectors die young. But the money's good.

Palmgrease. Smackers. Greenbacks. Wads. I widen my eyes
at a fortune; a set of knives on black cloth, shining,
utterly beautiful. Weep. The economy booms
like cannon, far out at sea on a lone ship. We leave   35
our places of work, tired, in the shortening hours, in the time
of night our town could be anywhere, and some of us pause
in the square, where a clown makes money swallowing fire.

Words, Wide Night

Somewhere on the other side of this wide night
and the distance between us, I am thinking of you.
The room is turning slowly away from the moon.

This is pleasurable. Or shall I cross that out and say
it is sad? In one of the tenses I singing   5
an impossible song of desire that you cannot hear.

La lala la. See? I close my eyes and imagine
the dark hills I would have to cross
to reach you. For I am in love with you and this

is what it is like or what it is like in words.   10

We Remember Your Childhood Well

Nobody hurt you. Nobody turned off the light and argued
with somebody else all night. The bad man on the moors
was only a movie you saw. Nobody locked the door.

Your questions were answered fully. No. That didn't occur.
You couldn't sing anyway, cared less. The moment's a
    blur, a *Film Fun*°   5
laughing itself to death in the coal fire. Anyone's guess.

Nobody forced you. You wanted to go that day. Begged.
    You chose
the dress. Here are the pictures, look at you. Look at us all,
smiling and waving, younger. The whole thing is inside
    your head.

What you recall are impressions; we have the facts. We
    called the tune.   10
The secret police of your childhood were older and wiser
    than you, bigger
than you. Call back the sound of their voices. Boom.
    Boom. Boom.

Nobody sent you away. That was an extra holiday, with people
you seemed to like. They were firm, there was nothing to fear.
There was none but yourself to blame if it ended in tears.   15

What does it matter now? No, no, nobody left the
    skidmarks of sin
on your soul and laid you wide open for Hell. You were loved.
Always. We did what was best. We remember your
    childhood well.

Litany

The soundtrack then was a litany – *candlewick*
bedspread three piece suite display cabinet –
and stiff-haired wives balanced their red smiles,
passing the catalogue. *Pyrex.* A tiny ladder
ran up Mrs Barr's American Tan leg, sly   5
like a rumour. Language embarrassed them.

The terrible marriages crackled, cellophane
round polyester shirts, and then The Lounge
would seem to bristle with eyes, hard
as the bright stones in engagement rings,   10
and sharp hands poised over biscuits as a word
was spelled out. An embarrassing word, broken

to bits, which tensed the air like an accident.
This was the code I learnt at my mother's knee, pretending
to read, where no one had cancer, or sex, or debts,   15
and certainly not leukaemia, which no one could spell.
The year a mass grave of wasps bobbed in a jam-jar;
a butterfly stammered itself in my curious hands.

A boy in the playground, I said, *told me*
to fuck off; and a thrilled, malicious pause   20
salted my tongue like an imminent storm. Then
uproar. *I'm sorry, Mrs Barr, Mrs Hunt, Mrs Emery,*
sorry, Mrs Raine. Yes, I can summon their names.
My mother's mute shame. The taste of soap.

Welltread

Welltread was Head and the Head's face was a fist. Yes,
I've got him. Spelling and Punishment. A big brass bell
dumb on his desk till only he shook it, and children
ran shrieking in the locked yard. Mr Welltread. Sir.

He meant well. They all did then. The loud, inarticulate dads, 5
the mothers who spat on hankies and rubbed you away.
But Welltread looked like a gangster. Welltread stalked
the forms, collecting thruppenny bits in a soft black hat.

We prayed for Aberfan,° vaguely reprieved. My socks dissolved,
two grey pools at my ankles, at the shock of my name 10
called out. The memory brings me to my feet
as a foul would. The wrong child for a trite crime.

And all I could say was *No*. Welltread straightened my hand
as though he could read the future there, then hurt himself
more than he hurt me. There was no cause for complaint. 15
There was the burn of a cane in my palm, still smouldering.

Confession

Come away into this dark cell and tell
your sins to a hidden man your guardian angel
works your conscience like a glove-puppet It
smells in here doesn't it does it smell
like a coffin how would you know C'mon   5
out with them sins those little maggoty things
that wriggle in the soul ... *Bless me Father ...*

Just how bad have you been there's no water
in hell merely to think of a wrong's as evil
as doing it ... *For I have sinned* ... Penance   10
will cleanse you like a bar of good soap so
say the words into the musty gloom aye
on your knees let's hear that wee voice
recite transgression in the manner approved ... *Forgive me ...*

You do well to stammer A proper respect   15
for eternal damnation see the flicker
of your white hands clasping each other like
Hansel and Gretel in the big black wood
cross yourself Remember the vinegar and sponge
there's light on the other side of the door ... *Mother*   20
of God ... if you can only reach it Jesus loves you.

The Good Teachers

You run round the back to be in it again.
No bigger than your thumbs, those virtuous women
size you up from the front row. Soon now,
Miss Ross will take you for double History.
You breathe on the glass, making a ghost of her, say   5
South Sea Bubble° Defenestration of Prague.°

You love Miss Pirie. So much, you are top
of her class. So much, you need two of you
to stare out from the year, serious, passionate.
The River's Tale by Rudyard Kipling by heart.   10
Her kind intelligent green eye. Her cruel blue one.
You are making a poem up for her in your head.

But not Miss Sheridan. Comment vous appelez.
But not Miss Appleby. Equal to the square
of the other two sides. Never Miss Webb.   15
Dar es Salaam. Kilimanjaro. Look. The good teachers
swish down the corridor in long, brown skirts,
snobbish and proud and clean and qualified.

And they've got your number. You roll the waistband
of your skirt over and over, all leg, all   20
dumb insolence, smoke-rings. You won't pass.
You could do better. But there's the wall you climb
into dancing, lovebites, marriage, the Cheltenham
and Gloucester, today. The day you'll be sorry one day.

First Love

Waking, with a dream of first love forming real words,
as close to my lips as lipstick, I speak your name,
after a silence of years, into the pillow, and the power
of your name brings me here to the window, naked,
to say it again to a garden shaking with light.   5

This was a child's love, and yet I clench my eyes
till the pictures return, unfocused at first, then
almost clear, an old film played at a slow speed.
All day I will glimpse it, in windows of changing sky,
in mirrors, my lover's eyes, wherever you are.   10

And later a star, long dead, here, seems precisely
the size of a tear. Tonight, a love-letter out of a dream
stammers itself in my heart. Such faithfulness.
You smile in my head on the last evening. Unseen
flowers suddenly pierce and sweeten the air.   15

Drunk

Suddenly the rain is hilarious.
The moon wobbles in the dusk.

What a laugh. Unseen frogs
belch in the damp grass.

The strange perfumes of darkening trees.   5
Cheap red wine

and the whole world a mouth.
Give me a double, a kiss.

Crush

The older she gets,
the more she awakes
with somebody's face strewn in her head
like petals which once made a flower.

What everyone does   5
is sit by a desk
and stare at the view, till the time
where they live reappears. Mostly in words.

Imagine a girl
turning to see   10
love stand by a window, taller,
clever, anointed with sudden light.

Yes, like an angel then,
to be truthful now.
At first a secret, erotic, mute;   15
today a language she cannot recall.

And we're all owed joy,
sooner or later.
The trick's to remember whenever
it was, or to see it coming.   20

Valentine

Not a red rose or a satin heart.

I give you an onion.
It is a moon wrapped in brown paper.
It promises light
like the careful undressing of love.   5

Here.
It will blind you with tears
like a lover.
It will make your reflection
a wobbling photo of grief.   10

I am trying to be truthful.

Not a cute card or a kissogram.

I give you an onion.
Its fierce kiss will stay on your lips,
possessive and faithful   15
as we are,
for as long as we are.

Take it.
Its platinum loops shrink to a wedding-ring,
if you like.   20
Lethal.
Its scent will cling to your fingers,
cling to your knife.

Mean Time

The clocks slid back an hour
and stole light from my life
as I walked through the wrong part of town,
mourning our love.

And, of course, unmendable rain   5
fell to the bleak streets
where I felt my heart gnaw
at all our mistakes.

If the darkening sky could lift
more than one hour from this day   10
there are words I would never have said
nor have heard you say.

But we will be dead, as we know,
beyond all light.
These are the shortened days   15
and the endless nights.

Fleur Adcock

Knife-play

All my scars are yours. We talk of pledges,
And holding out my hand I show
The faint burn on the palm and the hair-thin
Razor-marks at wrist and elbow:

Self-inflicted, yes; but your tokens –   5
Made as distraction from a more
Inaccessible pain than could have been
Caused by cigarette or razor –

And these my slightest marks. In all our meetings
You were the man with the long knives,   10
Piercing the living hopes, cutting connections,
Carving and dissecting motives,

And with an expert eye for dagger-throwing:
A showman's aim. Oh, I could dance
And dodge, as often as not, the whistling blades,   15
Turning on a brave performance

To empty stands. I leaned upon a hope
That this might prove to have been less
A gladiatorial show, contrived for murder,
Than a formal test of fitness   20

(Initiation rites are always painful)
To bring me ultimately to your
Regard. Well, in a sense it was; for now
I have found some kind of favour:

You have learnt softness; I, by your example,   25
Am well-schooled in contempt; and while
You speak of truce I laugh, and to your pleading
Turn a cool and guarded profile.

I have now, you might say, the upper hand:
These knives that bristle in my flesh   30
Increase my armoury and lessen yours.
I can pull out, whet and polish

Your weapons, and return to the attack,
Well-armed. It is a pretty trick,
But one that offers little consolation.   35
Such a victory would be Pyrrhic,°

Occurring when my strength is almost spent.
No: I would make an end of fighting
And, bleeding as I am from old wounds,
Die like the bee upon a sting.   40

For Andrew

'Will I die?' you ask. And so I enter on
The dutiful exposition of that which you
Would rather not know, and I rather not tell you.
To soften my 'Yes' I offer compensations –
Age and fulfilment ('It's so far away;   5
You will have children and grandchildren by then')
And indifference ('By then you will not care').
No need: you cannot believe me, convinced
That if you always eat plenty of vegetables
And are careful crossing the street you will live for ever.   10
And so we close the subject, with much unsaid –
This, for instance: Though you and I may die
Tomorrow or next year, and nothing remain
Of our stock, of the unique, preciously-hoarded
Inimitable genes we carry in us,   15
It is possible that for many generations
There will exist, sprung from whatever seeds,
Children straight-limbed, with clear enquiring voices,
Bright-eyed as you. Or so I like to think:
Sharing in this your childish optimism.   20

Regression

All the flowers have gone back into the ground.
We fell on them, and they did not lie
Crushed and crumpled, waiting to die
On the earth's surface. No: they suddenly wound

The film of their growth backwards. We saw them shrink   5
From blossom to bud to tiny shoot,
Down from the stem and up from the root.
Back to the seed, brothers. It makes you think.

Clearly they do not like us. They've gone away,
Given up. And who could blame   10
Anything else for doing the same?
I notice that certain trees look smaller today.

You can't escape the fact: there's a backward trend
From oak to acorn, and from pine
To cone; they all want to resign.   15
Understandable enough, but where does it end?

Harder, you'd think, for animals; yet the cat
Was pregnant, but has not produced.
Her rounded belly is reduced,
Somehow, to normal. How to answer that?   20

Buildings, perhaps, will be the next to go;
Imagine it: a tinkle of glass,
A crunch of brick, and a house will pass
Through the soil to the protest meeting below.

This whole conspiracy of inverted birth   25
Leaves only us; and how shall we
Endure as we deserve to be,
Foolish and lost on the naked skin of the earth?

Hauntings

Three times I have slept in your house
And this is definitely the last.
I cannot endure the transformations:
Nothing stays the same for an hour.

Last time there was a spiral staircase   5
Winding across the high room.
People tramped up and down it all night,
Carrying brief-cases, pails of milk, bombs,

Pretending not to notice me
As I lay in a bed lousy with dreams.   10
Couldn't you have kept them away?
After all, they were trespassing.

The time before it was all bathrooms,
Full of naked, quarrelling girls –
And you claim to like solitude: 15
I do not understand your arrangements.

Now the glass doors to the garden
Open on rows of stone columns;
Beside them stands a golden jeep.
Where are we this time? On what planet?   20

Every night lasts for a week.
I toss and turn and wander about,
Whirring from room to room like a moth,
Ignored by those indifferent faces.

At last I think I have woken up.   25
I lift my head from the pillow, rejoicing.
The alarm-clock is playing Schubert:
I am still asleep. This is too much.

Well, I shall try again in a minute.
I shall wake into this real room   30
With its shadowy plants and patterned screens
(Yes, I remember how it looks).

It will be cool, but I shan't wait
To light the gas-fire. I shall dress
(I know where my clothes are) and slip out.   35
You needn't think I am here to stay.

Happy Ending

After they had not made love
she pulled the sheet up over her eyes
until he was buttoning his shirt:
not shyness for their bodies – those
they had willingly displayed – but a frail   5
endeavour to apologise.

Later, though, drawn together by
a distaste for such 'untidy ends'
they agreed to meet again; whereupon
they giggled, reminisced, held hands   10
as though what they had made was love –
and not that happier outcome, friends.

Bogyman

Stepping down from the blackberry bushes
he stands in my path: Bogyman.
He is not as I had remembered him,
though he still wears the broad-brimmed hat,
the rubber-soled shoes and the woollen gloves.   5
No face; and that soft mooning voice
still spinning its endless distracting yarn.

But this is daylight, a misty autumn
Sunday, not unpopulated
by birds. I can see him in such colours   10
as he wears – fawn, grey, murky blue –
not all shadow-clothed, as he was that night
when I was ten; he seems less tall
(I have grown) and less muffled in silence.

I have no doubt at all, though, that he is   15
Bogyman. He is why children
do not sleep all night in their tree-houses.
He is why, when I had pleaded
to spend a night on the common, under
a cosy bush, and my mother   20
surprisingly said yes, she took no risk.

He was the risk I would not take; better
to make excuses, to lose face,
than to meet the really faceless, the one
whose name was too childish for us   25
to utter – 'murderers' we talked of, and
'lunatics escaped from Earlswood'.
But I met him, of course, as we all do.

Well, that was then; I survived; and later
survived meetings with his other   30
forms, bold or pathetic or disguised – the
slummocking figure in a dark
alley, or the lover turned suddenly
icy-faced; fingers at my throat
and ludicrous violence in kitchens.   35

I am older now, and (I tell myself,
circling carefully around him
at the far edge of the path, pretending
I am not in fact confronted)
can deal with such things. But what, Bogyman,   40
shall I be at twice my age? (At
your age?) Shall I be grandmotherly, fond

suddenly of gardening, chatty with
neighbours? Or strained, not giving in,
writing for *Ambit*◇ and hitch-hiking   45
to Turkey? Or sipping Guinness
in the Bald-Faced Stag, in wrinkled stockings? Or
(and now I look for the first time
straight at you) something like you, Bogyman?

A Game

They are throwing the ball
to and fro between them,
in and out of the picture.
She is in the painting
hung on the wall   5
in a narrow gold frame.
He stands on the floor
catching and tossing
at the right distance.
She wears a white dress,   10
black boots and stockings,
and a flowered straw hat.
She moves in silence
but it seems from her face
that she must be laughing.   15
Behind her is sunlight
and a tree-filled garden;
you might think to hear
birds or running water,
but no, there is nothing.   20
Once or twice he has spoken
but does so no more,
for she cannot answer.
So he stands smiling,
playing her game   25
(she is almost a child),
not daring to go,
intent on the ball.
And she is the same.
For what would result   30
neither wishes to know
if it should fall.

Earlswood

Air-raid shelters at school were damp tunnels
where you sang 'Ten Green Bottles' yet again
and might as well have been doing decimals.

At home, though, it was cosier and more fun:
cocoa and toast inside the Table Shelter,   5
our iron-panelled bunker, our new den.

By day we ate off it; at night you'd find us
under it, the floor plump with mattresses
and the wire grilles neatly latched around us.

You had to be careful not to bump your head;   10
we padded the hard metal bits with pillows,
then giggled in our glorious social bed.

What could be safer? What could be more romantic
than playing cards by torchlight in a raid?
Odd that it made our mother so neurotic   15

to hear the sirens; we were quite content –
but slightly cramped once there were four of us,
after we'd taken in old Mrs Brent

from down by the Nag's Head, who'd been bombed out.
She had her arm in plaster, but she managed   20
to dress herself, and smiled, and seemed all right.

Perhaps I just imagined hearing her
moaning a little in the night, and shaking
splinters of glass out of her long grey hair.

The next week we were sent to Leicestershire.   25

The Inner Harbour

Paua-Shell[◇]

Spilt petrol
oil on a puddle
the sea's colour-chart
porcelain, tie-dyed.
Tap the shell: 5
glazed calcium.

Cat's-Eye[◇]

Boss-eye, wall-eye, squinty lid
stony door for a sea-snail's tunnel

the long beach littered with them
domes of shell, discarded virginities   10

where the green girl wanders, willing
to lose hers to the right man

or to the wrong man, if he should raise
his frolic head above a sand dune

glossy-black-haired, and that smile on him   15

Sea-Lives

Under the sand at low tide
are whispers, hisses, long slithers,
bubbles, the suck of ingestion, a soft
snap: mysteries and exclusions.

Things grow on the dunes too –   20
pale straggle of lupin-bushes,
cutty-grass, evening primroses
puckering in the low light.

But the sea knows better.
Walk at the edge of its rich waves: 25
on the surface nothing shows;
underneath it is fat and fecund.

Shrimping-Net

Standing just under the boatshed
knee-deep in dappled water
sand-coloured legs and the sand itself   30
greenish in the lit ripples
watching the shrimps avoid her net
little flexible glass rockets
and the lifted mesh always empty
gauze and wire dripping sunlight   35

She is too tall to stand under
this house. It is a fantasy

And moving in from the bright outskirts
further under the shadowy floor
hearing a footstep creak above   40
her head brushing the rough timber
edging further bending her knees
creosote beams grazing her shoulder
the ground higher the roof lower
sand sifting on to her hair   45

She kneels in dark shallow water,
palms pressed upon shells and weed.

The Famous Traitor

His jailer trod on a rose-petal.
There were others on the stone floor.
His desk tidy; some lines in pencil,
the bible open.
    Years before
he'd lived like a private soldier –   5
a bag of nuts and the milk ration
for long days' marches. And under
the uniform a mathematician.
Puzzle-maker. After power:
which he got, this pastor's son   10
turned agnostic.
    The nature
of his 'new kind of treason',
his links with the Nazi high command,
the deals, the sense of mission,
are well-documented; and   15
beyond every explanation.

He died 'with dignity' some said;
some that he had to wait an hour,
died shivering in the bitter cold.
It looked like fear. It was fear: 20
or it was not. And he did,
or did not, shake hands before
that moment with the firing-squad.
Authorities let us down here.
His final audience, the 'crowd   25
of notables', might as well
have been, as he was, blindfold.
We are left with the empty cell
like a film-set; the table

where the man of action/dreamer   30
made notes on his father's bible
in a litter of roses. Enter
his faithful jailer, to record
just this. The rest remains obscure
like all that made a dictionary word   35
of his name; like what he did it for.

Prelude

Is it the long dry grass that is so erotic,
waving about us with hair-fine fronds of straw,
with feathery flourishes of seed, inviting us
to cling together, fall, roll into it
blind and gasping, smothered by stalks and hair,   5
pollen and each other's tongues on our hot faces?
Then imagine if the summer rain were to come,
heavy drops hissing through the warm air,
a sluice on our wet bodies, plastering us
with strands of delicious grass; a hum in our ears. 10

We walk a yard apart, talking
of literature and of botany.
We have known each other, remotely, for nineteen years.

The Ex-queen among the Astronomers

They serve revolving saucer eyes,
dishes of stars; they wait upon
huge lenses hung aloft to frame
the slow procession of the skies.

They calculate, adjust, record,   5
watch transits, measure distances.
They carry pocket telescopes
to spy through when they walk abroad.

Spectra possess their eyes; they face
upwards, alert for meteorites,   10
cherishing little glassy worlds:
receptacles for outer space.

But she, exile, expelled, ex-queen,
swishes among the men of science
waiting for cloudy skies, for nights   15
when constellations can't be seen.

She wears the rings he let her keep;
she walks as she was taught to walk
for his approval, years ago.
His bitter features taunt her sleep.   20

And so when these have laid aside
their telescopes, when lids are closed
between machine and sky, she seeks
terrestrial bodies to bestride.

She plucks this one or that among   25
the astronomers, and is become

his canopy, his occultation;
she sucks at earlobe, penis, tongue

mouthing the tubes of flesh; her hair
crackles, her eyes are comet-sparks.   30
She brings the distant briefly close
above his dreamy abstract stare.

On the Land

I'm still too young to remember how
I learned to mind a team of horses,
to plough and harrow: not a knack
you'd lose easily, once you had it.

It was in the Great War, that much-   5
remembered age. I was a landgirl
in my puttees and boots and breeches
and a round hat like a felt halo.

We didn't mind the lads laughing:
let them while they could, we thought,   10
they hadn't long. But it seemed long –
hay-making, and apple-picking,

and storing all those scented things
in sneezy dimness in the barn.
Then Jack turned seventeen and went,   15
and I knew Ted would go soon.

He went the week of Candlemas.°
After that it was all weather:
frosts and rains and spring and summer,
and the long days growing longer.   20

It rained for the potato harvest.
The front of my smock hung heavy
with claggy mud, from kneeling in it
mining for strays. Round segments

chopped clean off by the blade   25
flashed white as severed kneecaps.
I grubbed for whole ones, baby skulls
to fill my sack again and again.

When the pain came, it wouldn't
stop. I couldn't stand. I dropped   30
the sack and sank into a trench.
Ethel found me doubled up.

Mr Gregson took me home,
jolting on the back of the wagon.
I tossed and writhed on my hard bed,   35
my head hunched into the bolster,

dreaming of how if just for once,
for half an hour, the knobbly mattress
could turn into a billow of clouds
I might be able to get to sleep.   40

For Heidi with Blue Hair

When you dyed your hair blue
(or, at least, ultramarine
for the clipped sides, with a crest
of jet-black spikes on top)
you were sent home from school   5

because, as the headmistress put it,
although dyed hair was not
specifically forbidden, yours
was, apart from anything else,
not done in the school colours.   10

Tears in the kitchen, telephone-calls
to school from your freedom-loving father:
'She's not a punk in her behaviour;
it's just a style.' (You wiped your eyes,
also not in a school colour.)   15

'She discussed it with me first –
we checked the rules.' 'And anyway, Dad,
it cost twenty-five dollars.
Tell them it won't wash out –
not even if I wanted to try.'   20

It would have been unfair to mention
your mother's death, but that
shimmered behind the arguments.
The school had nothing else against you;
the teachers twittered and gave in.   25

Next day your black friend had hers done
in grey, white and flaxen yellow –
the school colours precisely:
an act of solidarity, a witty
tease. The battle was already won.   30

Chippenham

The maths master was eight feet tall.
He jabbed his clothes'-prop arm at me
halfway across the classroom, stretched
his knobbly finger, shouted 'You!

You're only here one day in three,   5
and when you are you might as well
not be, for all the work you do!
What do you think you're playing at?'

What did I think? I shrank into
my grubby blouse. Who did I think   10
I was, among these blazered boys,
these tidy girls in olive serge?

My green skirt wasn't uniform:
clothes were on coupons, after all.
I'd get a gymslip – blue, not green –   15
for Redhill Grammar, some time soon

when we went home. But, just for now,
what did I think? I thought I was
betrayed. I thought of how I'd stood
an hour waiting for the bus   20

that morning, by a flooded field,
watching the grass-blades drift and sway
beneath the water like wet hair;
hoping for Mrs Johnson's call:

'Jean, are you there? The clock was wrong.   25
You've missed the bus.' And back I'd run

to change my clothes, be Jean again,
play with the baby, carry pails

of water from the village tap,
go to the shop, eat toast and jam,   30
and then, if she could shake enough
pennies and farthings from her bag,

we might get to the pictures. But
the clock was fast, it seemed, not slow;
the bus arrived; and as I slid   35
anonymously into it

an elegant male prefect said
'Let Fleur sit down, she's got bad feet.'
I felt my impetigo° scabs
blaze through my shoes. How did he know?   40

The Prize-winning Poem

It will be typed, of course, and not all in capitals: it will
                          use upper and lower case
in the normal way; and where a space is usual it will have
                          a space.
It will probably be on white paper, or possibly blue, but
                          almost certainly not pink.
It will not be decorated with ornamental scroll-work in
                          coloured ink,
nor will a photograph of the poet be glued above his or her
                          name,   5
and still less a snap of the poet's children frolicking in a
                          jolly game.
The poem will not be about feeling lonely and being fifteen
and unless the occasion of the competition is a royal
                          jubilee it will not be about the queen.
It will not be the first poem the author has written in his
                          life
and will probably not be about the death of his daughter,
                          son or wife   10
because although to write such elegies fulfils a therapeutic
                          need
in large numbers they are deeply depressing for the judges
                          to read.
The title will not be 'Thoughts' or 'Life' or 'I Wonder Why'
or 'The Bunny-rabbit's Birthday Party' or 'In Days of
                          Long Gone By'.
'Tis and 'twas, o'er and e'er, and such poetical
                          contractions will not be found   15
in the chosen poem. Similarly clichés will not abound:

dawn will not herald another bright new day, nor dew
                           sparkle like diamonds in a dell,
nor trees their arms upstretch. Also the poet will be able
                                   to spell.
Large meaningless concepts will not be viewed with
                          favour: myriad is out;
infinity is becoming suspect; aeons and galaxies are in
                              some doubt. 20
Archaisms and inversions will not occur; nymphs will not
                         their fate bemoan.
Apart from this there will be no restrictions upon the style
                              or tone.
What is required is simply the masterpiece we'd all write
                             if we could.
There is only one prescription for it: it's got to be good.

Mary Magdalene° and the Birds

1
Tricks and tumbles are my trade; I'm
all birds to all men.
I switch voices, adapt my features,
do whatever turn you fancy.
All that is constant is my hair: 5

plumage, darlings, beware of it.

2
Blackbird: that's the one to watch –
or he is, with his gloss and weapon.
Not a profession for a female,
his brown shadow. Thrush is better,   10
cunning rehearser among the leaves,
and speckle-breasted, maculate.

3

A wound of some kind. All that talk
of the pelican, self-wounding,
feeding his brood from an ever-bleeding 15
bosom turns me slightly sick.

But seriousness can light upon
the flightiest. This tingling ache,
nicer than pain, is a blade-stroke:
not my own, but I let it happen. 20

4

What is balsam? What is nard?
Sweetnesses from the sweet life,
obsolete, fit only for wasting.

I groom you with this essence. Wash it
down the drain with tears and water. 25
We are too human. Let it pass.

5

With my body I thee worship:
breast on stone lies the rockdove
cold on that bare nest, cooing
its low call, unlulled, 30
restless for the calling to cease.

6

Mary Magdalene sang in the garden.
It was a swansong, said the women,
for his downdrift on the river.

It sounded more of the spring curlew 35
or a dawn sky full of larks,
watery trillings you could drown in.

RESOURCE NOTES

Who has written these poems and why?

Liz Lochhead

Liz Lochhead was born in 1947, in the west of Scotland, not far from Glasgow. She grew up in a little mining village on the edge of the moors, which she describes as 'countryside, but very industrially-scarred countryside'. The community was characterised by its division into Protestant and Catholic villages with their own separate schools and churches, which, according to Liz Lochhead, gave her 'a terrible, divisive upbringing'. Her parents were Protestant Scots but 'very unbigoted – they weren't interested in sectarian differences'.

She attended Glasgow School of Art, where she studied drawing and painting, but has said that 'halfway through Art School, my real love switched to writing'. She qualified in 1970 and joined a writer's workshop whilst working as an art teacher. She gave her first public poetry reading in 1972, at a poetry festival in Edinburgh, where she learnt the vital importance of performance, and the power this can have on an audience. As well as poetry writing, Liz Lochhead began to write dramatic monologues, revues, performance pieces and stage plays. She has said about the difference between poetry and play writing, 'that writing for the theatre is so practical, quite vulgar, quite rough … whereas poetry is very much about getting the right voice and tone, and tinkering.'

Since 1978, Liz Lochhead has been a full-time writer living on writer's exchange fellowships, taking posts as writer-in-residence at several universities, and travelling the country doing poetry performances. She rejects the term 'feminist-writer' – 'at least in that hyphenated fashion since you might as well call me a wee, fat, brown-haired writer … But of course I am a feminist and as such perhaps I take greater care of the female characters in my poems and don't short-change them.'

✦ Activity

A number of Liz Lochhead's poems and performance pieces included in this collection adopt the persona and voice of a fictitious character, for example:

- 'Almost Miss Scotland' (p. 10);
- 'Six Men Monologues' (p. 26);
- 'Meeting Norma Nimmo' (p. 13);
- 'Favourite Shade' (p. 31).

Write a poem or short piece of prose in the same style as **one** of these, in which you write in the persona of Liz Lochhead – about being a professional poet. To prepare for this, look at the kind of poetry she writes and the brief biography above to form some impressions of what she is like.

Jackie Kay

Jackie Kay, the youngest poet in this collection, was born in 1961. She was adopted and brought up in Glasgow. She has written about the experience of being a black child in a predominantly white country in *The Adoption Papers*, where she has said, 'I've used my own experience as a springboard to create the book.'

The Adoption Papers tells the story of the daughter's search for her birth mother, and the adoptive mother's search for a child. It is not strictly autobiographical, but rather, is created out of a real life. Jackie's parents were members of the Communist Party, and their interests in such diverse people as Nelson Mandela, Paul Robeson, Angela Davis and Bessie Smith influenced Kay's poetry. So too has the experience of racism in Scotland, vividly depicted in *The Adoption Papers*.

Jackie Kay went to school in Glasgow. Her English teacher once sent her to see the then writer in residence, Alasdair Gray, who was tremendously encouraging. She found the experience of growing up in a city where the presence of a great many Scottish writers – Liz Lochhead, Tom Leonard, James Kelman, and Alasdair Gray, to name a few – was exciting and inspirational. She often attended 'Poetry and Pints' nights as a teenager, and enjoyed the socialising aspect of poetry. Poetry attracted her not just because of the ways it stretches language, but because it could be enjoyed publicly and privately, combining as it does elements of drama and song. She has said that, 'folk songs and blues are as big an influence on my work as the work of other writers.'

As a child, Jackie Kay went part time to the Royal Academy of Music and Drama, where she greatly enjoyed improvising and acting. She then went to Stirling University and read English. She has written several plays for various companies including Gay Sweatshop, The Sphinx and 7:84. Her work is often about people who live on the margins, who have complex identities, and who face society's prejudices.

✦ Activities

1 *The Adoption Papers* was first broadcast on Radio 3 in August 1990. Imagine that the BBC has decided to broadcast the poem as a play once again. *Radio Times* has commissioned you to write a short article (about 300 words), in which you introduce the poem to the audience, and include snippets of an interview you have conducted with Jackie Kay.

   To prepare for this, look at examples of articles of this type from publications such as *TV Times* and *Radio Times*. How will you aim to arouse the reader's interest? How much will you make of the autobiographical links between Kay's life and the poem?

2 Write an autobiographical poem of your own which incorporates and interweaves three voices: yours, and those of two people who are or have been important in your life. Perhaps focus on an incident or a situation which has made a lasting impression on you, or which has had a significant effect on your life.

Re-read *The Adoption Papers* carefully to get ideas for the style, voice and layout of your own poem. See, for example, 'Chapter 1: The Seed' for a model of how the voices of three characters might interweave.

Carol Ann Duffy

Carol Ann Duffy was born in Glasgow in 1955. She grew up in Staffordshire, the daughter of left-wing working-class Catholics. She went to a convent school run by a French order of nuns; later she attended a girls' grammar school. She describes the teaching in both schools as 'excellent'. As a member of a Catholic family, she went to church every Sunday and Communion every week. The other influence on family life was the Labour Party – her father stood as Labour candidate at Leigh in Lancashire in the 1983 general election. Duffy herself is not a member of a political party: 'I don't like joining things – I like being an outsider.'

At sixteen, she published a pamphlet of poems, with the help of her English teacher. After reading philosophy at Liverpool University, she wrote a couple of stage plays, which were performed at the Playhouse, and TV scripts for Granada television. Meanwhile she began to publish her poems with small presses and in magazines. Most of her poetry has been published by Anvil Press, a small publishing house in London.

Today, she lives in London as a freelance writer, and gives poetry readings at schools, community centres and conferences around the country. She descibes herself as a feminist and thinks that 'men should be encouraged to be feminists'. Her many love poems address both hetero- and homosexual audiences. She is now one of Britain's leading poets and has won a number of national poetry awards.

✦ *Activity*

When poets give public readings of their poems, they must select the titles, range, number and order of the poems they are going to read according to the type of audience (and perhaps, venue). If you were to make this choice for Carol Ann Duffy, which poems would you pick? Plan a list of titles in your chosen order, for a half-hour poetry reading for **two** of the following:

- an A-level class at a girls' grammar school;
- a GCSE group at a mixed comprehensive school;
- an English teachers' conference held at a university;
- a writers' workshop of adults of mixed ages.

In preparing for this, consider two things. First, what stereotypical assumptions might you be making about these groups of people? Second, from what you have learnt about Carol Ann Duffy from reading her poems and the biography above, do you think she would go along with such assumptions? To help you answer this, read 'Head of English' (p. 62), where she describes her experience of giving a poetry reading at a girls' school, in the persona of this teacher.

Fleur Adcock

Fleur Adcock was born in 1934 in Papakura, New Zealand. As a child, she lived in New Zealand and later in England, where she attended eleven different schools: 'We moved around a lot … and each time I didn't have any friends so I retreated to an interior world.' Fleur and her sister were 'sent off to the country to live on a farm' where there was 'no television, so there were drawings and games and telling yourself stories in your head and writing these down'.

In 1947, just after the Second World War, her family returned to New Zealand where, as a teenager, she began writing her first poems. When she was 17 she went to Victoria University in Wellington, where she met and married the poet Alistair Campbell. She describes how his fame as a poet 'daunted' her and so she stopped writing for a time, 'perhaps I was inhibited by being married to a real poet; or perhaps I was too busy, first as a married student, then as a student and mother.' She and her husband divorced when she was 24, and, soon after this, she began to write seriously, encouraged by a group of fellow poets.

She emigrated to England in 1963, glad to escape New Zealand which she found 'stifling'. In comparison, she felt that England was both 'exciting' and 'a culture shock'. For fifteen years she worked as a librarian, broken by one year off when she took a Fellowship at a teachers' college in the Lake District. This led to further arts grants and enabled her to become a freelance writer. She describes herself as 'a poet before I was a woman poet … and I didn't think of myself as any different from a male poet until I discovered I was'.

✦ *Activity*

After reading Fleur Adcock's poems in this collection, and the biography above, select four poems which seem to you to represent different stages in the poet's life. For example, if you were to identify the first stage as 'at school', which poem might you pick to represent it?

Compare notes with other members of your group to see which stages and poems you have chosen, and why.

✦

What type of texts are these poems?

There are many genres writers can choose for expressing their ideas, ranging from 'fictional' genres such as poetry, the novel, the short story, the dramatic monologue and the play, to 'non-fictional' genres like biography, reportage and the essay. Of the four poets in this collection, three – Liz Lochhead, Jackie Kay and Carol Ann Duffy – have also written plays. Indeed, certain poems, such as Kay's *The Adoption Papers*, have been dramatised as radio plays, and other pieces in this collection, such as Lochhead's 'Six Men Monologues' or 'Meeting Norma Nimmo', might be said to cross the boundary between poem and play – in the form of dramatic monologue.

Why do writers choose poetry as the medium for expressing particular ideas? What is it about the type of text a poem is that gives poets the power to express these ideas? How do poems, read aloud, differ from performance pieces? The following section gives snippets from interviews with the poets in this collection about their views on the medium of poetry: its attractions; the difference between performance poetry and poetry written for the printed page; and the notion of 'women's poetry' – whether female poets perceive that they are writing a different kind of poetry from male poets.

On the attraction of poetry

> I write much less poetry than I used to, but when I do it, it's my favourite thing I do. I wish I wrote more. I hope it won't go away. It's the most satisfying thing to write ... A play is something that doesn't exist when you have written it. It only exists when it begins to be performed. Whereas a poem is something that even before you have tightened it up properly, once you've got it finished, even if it is lying under your bed, there it is: it's a *thing*. That's what satisfies me the most about poetry, that it is not for anything whatsoever and that you don't really do it to order.
>
> (Liz Lochhead, *Verse*, vol 8, no 2)

Poetry is very private; you make your own decisions without anyone hanging over your shoulder throwing things out. As a playwright, other people like the director and actors have to be involved, and it can be upsetting and even traumatic to come to rehearsals and see everyone fighting over lines you wrote and which have meaning for you.

(Jackie Kay, *The Scotsman*, 1993)

On the merits of printed and performance poetry

I write primarily for the printed page, not for performance ... I am writing for my own satisfaction to a certain extent, but also I write in proper sentences because I want the poetry to be readable again and again. Performance poetry is something you hear once and don't need to hear again. I regard that as rather trivial. Primarily I write to be between covers – for books – so that people can go back and read them again, and see all the levels they have missed in the performance.

(Fleur Adcock, *Acumen*, 1992)

Well, *The Adoption Papers* is drama really, it's much more drama than one long poem. Really it needs to be heard as much as it needs to be read. I'm sure people can make a job of reading it on the page ... but they get confused by the different typefaces and I don't know that it works as well on the page as it works to hear it.

(Jackie Kay, interview with Patrick Williams, 1994)

Although I was very nervous about appearing in public at first, especially when I was younger, I now feel that poetry readings are an essential part of the life of poetry in this country. They offer something more vivid, more direct than the reading of the text.

(Carol Ann Duffy to Judith Baxter, 1994)

If you are going to [read] in public, I think you ought to decide the selection of poems which will be accessible to an audience, you ought to do it loud enough so they can hear you and you ought to make some sort of communication with them.

(Liz Lochhead, *Verse*, vol 8, no 2)

I see a very clear distinction between my poems and and my performance pieces. For me they are quite different forms.

(Liz Lochhead to Judith Baxter, 1994)

On the notion of women's poetry

I don't like the way that bookshops segregate women, put them in the 'women's section' instead of the 'poetry section'. I think they are poets; but I feel that the fact that they are women poets needs or needed, to be drawn to the attention because a lot of poets were being overlooked at a certain phase in our literary history. I think that's not the case now. I think that women can stop having all these women's anthologies. But women, young women, particularly students, who are beginning to read poetry want to be able to find women, look them out. And an anthology is one way of helping that to happen.

(Fleur Adcock, *Acumen*, 1992)

I don't mind being called a feminist poet, but I wouldn't mind if I wasn't. I think the concerns of art go beyond that. I think as long as the work is read it really doesn't matter what the cover is. I have never in my life sat down and thought 'I will write a feminist poem' ... It also comes back to – and this is a sort of vanity – the things women can and can't do.

(Carol Ann Duffy, *Bête Noire*, 1988)

Well, I think you see the same problem again and again, often in female poets. If you think of Sylvia Plath, she actually had to invent this language to describe the state she was in because she had internalised all the male and literary and high art models, and she had internalised them so that they were her. I mean that they are not something false. It's something that you own, this male half. So for me if I think about it, I had already got a posh, grown-up male English voice to write in. Although that wasn't the voice I spoke in. And probably [my poetry] was about articulating that voice into being Scottish, female.

(Liz Lochhead, *Verse*, vol 8)

✦ *Activities*

1 What is your definition of poetry?

In a pair, read the four works suggested below (which all, to varying degrees, test the boundary between definitions of poetry and other literary genres):

- *The Adoption Papers* by Jackie Kay (p. 34);
- 'Six Men Monologues' by Liz Lochhead (p. 26);
- 'Translating the English' by Carol Ann Duffy (p. 70);
- 'The Prize-winning Poem' by Fleur Adcock (p. 106).

Discuss each of the pieces according to the statements you have written, aiming to agree on which texts qualify as poetry, and which are less easy to categorise.

Join with another pair to share and exchange your findings. How much agreement is there between you? Which of these pieces could be easily adapted to another medium (for example, a short story; a speech from a play; part of a radio play; part of a documentary), which less so?

2 Printed page or performance?

Poetry may be written both for the printed page and for performance – either read aloud or performed aloud to an audience. There are many examples of poems in this collection which lend themselves to a dramatic performance. Carry out one or more of the following (it would be useful if you could have photocopies of the poems you are studying, to mark up).

a For any of the poems:

In small groups, work out how you might read the poem aloud. How much help does the poem give you on the printed page as to the way it should be read?

Work out a reading of the poem to include all your voices. Mark up your photocopy to indicate such things as:

- stress – which words or phrases you wish to emphasise;
- pauses – where you will leave a pause;
- volume – where you will read more quietly or loudly;
- pace – where you will read more quickly or slowly.

b For Fleur Adcock and one other:

Fleur Adcock has said that she primarily writes for the printed page, whereas other poets in the collection (see Liz Lochhead above), are aware of how their poems must engage a live audience. Choose one poem by Fleur Adcock, and one poem (or part of a poem) by another poet in this collection. In pairs, work out how you might perform the poem to an audience, using any indications the poems themselves give you as to the way they should be read. For example, note the use of such things as:

- punctuation (or lack of it);
- line length;
- shape of each stanza (verse);
- use of different typefaces (for example *italics*, **bold**).

Perform (or read aloud) the two poems to an audience (your class or a small group). Afterwards discuss the following:

- Which poem was easier to adapt and why?
- Which poem worked better in performance?
- Should poets make an effort to indicate on the page how their poems should work in performance?

c For Jackie Kay

In small groups, work out how you might adapt (part of) *The Adoption Papers* for a radio performance.

How much help does the poem give you about the way it might be read? (Consider the use of punctuation, line length, shape of the verse, different typefaces.)

On a photocopy, add any directions you think important about the use of, for example:

- voice – to express the personalities of the three different characters;
- sound effects;
- moments of tension or relief.

After your performance (which you might tape record), discuss:

- How easily did the poem lend itself to being adapted to radio?
- How limited or extensive were the directions your group had to add?
- What do you feel are some of the differences between reading a poem like *The Adoption Papers* on the page, and then 'off the page' in performance?

3 Women's poetry

Carol Ann Duffy has spoken about the notion of a 'feminist poem'. What do you understand by this expression? Is it used neutrally, or as a compliment or as a kind of insult? What kind of a text is a 'feminist poem'?

Choose **two** of the poets in the collection and make a catalogue of the subjects or issues covered in their poems. To what extent is there a distinction between the notion of a 'feminist poem' and Liz Lochhead's notion of a poem written in a female voice?

◆

How were these poems produced?

When you read a printed poem in the pages of an anthology like this one, it may not occur to you to ask how the poem came to be there. If the poet comes to your school or college to give a reading, and gives you the chance to ask questions afterwards, you might well ask, 'Where do you get your ideas from?' or, 'How did you become a professional poet?'

The process by which a poem first gets written and then eventually gets published in a collection of poetry is neither simple nor obvious. Many poems written by talented poets probably never get published. The ones you may be asked to read or study are the survivors of an extraordinary system which begins with the poet's initial ideas and ends with critical approval from academics, journalists, literary critics, teachers, examiners and students. The work of both Carol Ann Duffy and Fleur Adcock has appeared on A-level examination sylla-buses, and yet, ironically, both have written poems critical of school life. The following section, which draws on extracts from interviews with Duffy and Adcock, traces the process by which poems arrive in an anthology like *Four Women Poets*.

Getting ideas for writing

Although there is a popular myth that poets gain inspiration 'from the ether', it may also be true to say that there are other, less mysterious sources and influences: their own experiences, for example of school and childhood; their experience and use of language; people they have known; the work of other poets and writers; and the complex world in which they live.

> What I am doing is living in the twentieth century in Britain and listening to the radio news every day and reading the newspapers every day and meeting people who've had wonderful or horrifying experiences, and sometimes that will nudge me towards a poem.
>
> (Carol Ann Duffy, *Bête Noire*, 6, 1988)

You may not think school is much of a subject for a poem but we spend an awful lot of our lives in school and it is the first real experience we get of mixing with people outside the family and having to adjust to the ways of an institution. Going to a new school always made my heart sink and my stomach turn over, but for various reasons I went to rather a lot of them ... so there came a time much later in my life when I thought I'd like to write about that feeling of being an outsider, being a new girl and the one who didn't know anybody and didn't really belong. I wrote a group of poems about my eleven schools in England.

(Fleur Adcock, *Writers on Tape*, 1994)

All writers draw on their own experience and a lot of my experience has been heightened. My life provides me with constant things to write about, though what interests me is the point at which that experience intersects with the reader's own feelings.

(Jackie Kay, *The Scotsman*, 1993)

Starting to write a poem

You may have been asked to write a poem or a story as a student, and found the process of getting started the hardest part. How do professional writers go about it? Is there any similarity at all with your own experience?

It starts with with a line or a phrase, but it always begins with the sound of it. Some people begin with a visual image ... But for me it's something I hear my voice saying. Sometimes something quite mad – a phrase from a dream; when I wake up I jot it down. Then it goes on to attach itself to whatever are my preoccupations at the time, and I realise that the phrase has some connection with the subject, and it begins to turn into a poem. I don't know always where it is going to lead me; the end is often not in view when I begin. It's a process of slowly extracting the poem from my subconscious, where I sometimes feel it's lurking, ready-made and waiting to be discovered.

(Fleur Adcock, *Verse*, vol 10)

Other poets begin with a city, or a landscape, an idea or a concept, but I really begin with a voice – that's what starts me off with everything I write – an imagined voice, it doesn't need to be a real voice. What I am trying to capture is a language, a way that a character speaks, and make it say much more than it does.

(Jackie Kay, interview with Patrick Williams, 1994)

Writing and rewriting

Few poets are able to write their poems straight off, in a moment of inspiration, and know that it is ready for performance or publication – although there are always exceptions to this. Most poets write several drafts of a poem before they are completely satisfied. Carol Ann Duffy, for example, has said that a single poem might, in its last stages, take over a month – sometimes as long as two months – to resolve itself fully:

> I do rewrite but I hope that the language that I use is the language of my time, the late twentieth century. It isn't more poetic or separate from the language in which we think, speak or read. The raw material is immediately there because it's how we are talking now, then I rewrite.
>
> (Carol Ann Duffy, *Writers' Monthly*, October 1993)

Getting poetry published

For many poets there is a prescribed route into print, publishing poems first with small presses and in pamphlets, submitting to specialist magazines and competitions, then giving poetry readings and workshops. Usually it takes time to complete enough poems for an anthology, but once a poet has a full collection, they might approach the more well-known publishing houses.

Carol Ann Duffy has spoken about the difficulties for women writers in particular in getting accepted and promoted by the large, established publishers. She has so far published all her poetry volumes with Anvil Press – a small publishing company:

I've stayed with them because they've got qualities you perhaps
don't get in the big publishers. They're personal and consult
you about typeface, the paper and the cover. I have a very good
relationship with the editor there ... Most of the publishing
houses have male editors. There's one female poetry editor in
Britain. Most of the reviewers are male; most of the
anthologists are too. There is a two-tier thing but this is
changing at grass roots level and has yet to filter through to the
boys.

(Carol Ann Duffy, *Writers' Monthly*, October 1993)

Getting poetry into school

The study of poets in schools and colleges used to be drawn
from a highly select group of established, literary figures from
the past who were usually male. Today, you are also likely to
study poetry by contemporary, recently published writers,
some of whom may be young and female. However, there is
still some kind of a 'vetting system'. There is still a number of
informal 'qualifications' a poet must have for their work to be
nominated as a set text for examinations, or indeed to be
chosen as a coursework text for class or home study (see
Activity 2 on page 125).

For a writer or text to be chosen for educational study, they
must become 'visible'. One way this happens is through reviews in the national press, such as this one about Jackie Kay
from *The Guardian* in 1991:

Kay's first collection of poems *Adoption Papers* [sic], is
published today. Sections of the book have already been
produced as a radio play and earned her the 1990 Eric Gregory
Award: she has already written four plays and contributed to
several anthologies. Alistair Niven, Director of Literature at the
Arts Council, describes Kay as 'one of Britain's most promising
voices in poetry'.

✦ *Activities:*

1 At poetry readings, poets often introduce the pieces they are about to read to their audience, saying where the ideas came from, setting the piece in its context or background and saying how it came to be written. When you read a poem or performance piece on the page, you can only guess at such information.

Choose any work from this collection which you have enjoyed, and implies an interesting background (the four below are given as suggestions only). Imagine, and then write, the introduction that the poet might have told her audience at a poetry reading:

- 'Almost Miss Scotland' by Liz Lochhead (p. 10);
- 'Originally' by Carol Ann Duffy (p. 67);
- *The Adoption Papers* by Jackie Kay (p. 34);
- 'For Heidi with Blue Hair' by Fleur Adcock (p. 103).

2 In pairs, look at the biographical details of each of the four poets on pages 109–114. Draw up a list of the 'qualifications' each poet appears to have achieved for possible selection by teachers and examiners for:

- coursework study, either at GCSE or A-level;
- examination study, either at GCSE or A-level.

What is your view of such 'qualifications' or criteria? Is there any kind of poetry you would wish to add to the current repertoire? Are there kinds of poetry which should be given **more** (or perhaps **less**) emphasis?

✦

How do these poems (and performance pieces) present their subject?

There can be no common answer to this question when you apply it to the works of four poets writing in differing styles on a range of subjects. This section aims to outline some of the broad hallmarks of each poet's style of writing, and to encourage you to read, and re-read, their work to discover further answers to the question in the title above.

Liz Lochhead

Voice
She uses the voices of a wide range of individuals, often in the form of dramatic monologue.

Make a note of the different kinds of characters Lochhead uses as mouthpieces for her poems and performance pieces. Are there any links or connections between the kinds of characters she chooses to portray?

Satire
She does wry 'send-ups' of a range of characters and subjects: the female condition, the British male, the imperial history of Britain, Scottishness, the banalities of everyday life and more.

How does Lochhead make fun of her subject and yet at the same time make a serious point? Consider any piece where you feel that she is having fun at the expense of her subject and yet allowing that character to express something important.

Conversational speech rhythms
She uses various kinds of speech rhythms in her work, from Glaswegian working-class dialects to Standard English spoken with the rhythms of Scottish speech. She aims to represent the

myriad ways of speaking she believes is essentially a Scottish phenomenon: 'Scots is a fantastic language for multiplicity of register.'

Note some of the ways in which she recreates Scottish speech in her work, including:

- colloquialisms – slang, clichés, swear words, common expressions;
- phonetic transcriptions – words written down as they sound in a Glaswegian accent;
- references to popular culture – advertising, personalities, news;
- direct speech.

Free verse form

She mainly uses an unstructured verse form in this collection (that is, no formal, set use of rhythm or rhyme), but allows the content of the piece partly to determine the form. However, she is also well-known for using more formal structures such as metre and rhyming couplets, particularly for her comedic verse. In this collection, there are one or two examples of more formal use (see, for example, 'Con-densation' on page 19, where she uses a form of quatrain – a stanza of four lines, usually with alternate rhymes).

Re-read 'Meeting Norma Nimmo' (p. 13), and work out how you might transform this from a prose monologue into a poem using free form:

- What will you include?
- What will you leave out?
- How will you re-arrange the shape to give it the rhythm and 'feel' of a poem?

Once you have adapted it, reflect on how far you think that the **form** of the poem alters the **sense** of the original prose piece.

Jackie Kay

Voice

She interweaves three dramatic interior monologues, each one representing the voice of a different character – the birth mother, the adoptive mother and the daughter of both. This technique allows the reader to enter and share the thought processes of each character.

Is there any exchange of speech or thoughts between the three characters? What is the effect of interweaving their separate thought processes?

How are the voices of the **other** characters in the poem revealed? For example, the social worker, the school teacher, the other children at the school?

Story-telling techniques

She draws upon a range of story-telling techniques commonly found in prose and fiction. Can you add to this list?
- the use of chapters;
- the use of time markers to indicate the passage of time in a narrative, for example:
  - 'When I got home;'
  - 'A week later I stood at my window;'
  - 'Later that same night' (from Chapter 4).

How does the poem differ from a conventional story:
- in the way it looks?
- in the way it sounds?

Conversational speech rhythms

She uses the rhythms and expressions of direct, everyday speech in places, drawing on clichés, popular expressions, fragments of speech and slang, to give realism to the character's thoughts and experiences:
- 'I knee him in the balls. What was that?'

- 'My fist is steel. I punch and punch his gut.'
- 'Sorry I didn't hear you?' (from Chapter 7).

'Poetic' description

In contrast to the above, she uses on occasions rich, colourful and almost sensuous descriptions with a lyrical rhythm:

- 'Olubayo was the colour of peat
  when we walked out heads turned
  like horses, folk stood like trees ...' (from Chapter 7).

Select any chapter and highlight with a marker pen (on a photocopy) any lines which you would consider to be 'poetically descriptive'. With a different colour pen, highlight any lines which you would call 'conversational'. Can you explain any links between a particular speaker and a particular style of language?

Carol Ann Duffy

Voice

She uses the voices of a wide range of characters, and, like Liz Lochhead, often in the form of dramatic monologue.

What do you notice about the kind of characters Duffy chooses to portray? How do they compare with the range of characters in Liz Lochhead's dramatic monologues?

Everyday language

She uses the expressions and speech rhythms of everyday conversation – clichés, popular expressions, fragments of speech, slang, references to news, television and advertising.

Particularly notice Duffy's use of *italics* in poems. She often highlights inane clichés and pithy little phrases in italics. Why does she do this?

Musicality of the rhythm

Duffy has said, 'I can have the rhythm of a whole poem in my head and no words. And it isn't music and it isn't language; it's something in between.'

In groups, choose a poem where you feel there is a strong, almost musical rhythm and set it to music in a way that brings out its inherent rhythm. You might do this by using percussion instruments such as drums, tambourines and triangles; or by drawing on the talents of members of your group who play band or orchestral instruments.

Visual images

She makes use of strong, visual images, either literally as the subject matter of the poem (see, for example, 'Standing Female Nude' (p. 65), which is about the material world of art objects), or in the form of visual imagery – as similes and, more often, metaphors:

- 'The clocks slid back an hour
  and stole light from my life' (from 'Mean Time', page 84)

What do you think about Duffy's assessment of herself as 'a poet of the ear rather than the eye'?

Fleur Adcock

Formal verse

Some of Adcock's poems are influenced by the conventions of formal verse where there may be a set metre (a form of rhythm where there is a regular number of stresses in each line of verse) and/or a rhyming scheme. She has said that she writes for the printed page rather than performance, and is attracted by the formal properties of poetry: ' There's always at least a regular rhythm count – four stresses per line or some sort of shape, which may only come across when I read it aloud. There are a lot of quatrains which are pretty regular except that they don't rhyme a lot.'

Find examples of Adcock's use of quatrains in this collection of her poems. What does the quatrain form add to these particular poems?

Free verse

There are also several examples of poems in this collection written in free verse – where there is no set rhythm or rhyming scheme. But this does not make it an easy option for poets. Adcock has spoken about how difficult free verse is to write and believes it is more challenging than formal verse: 'I think my most profound utterances come out in free verse of some kind. I tend to use strict forms when I am writing something light.'

Look at the range of Adcock's poems in this collection and group them under two headings – formal verse and free verse. Are there any which you find difficult to categorise? Does Adcock's description of the relationship between her subjects and the style of verse hold true here?

Ironic detachment

She tends to write about subjects with a sense of distance and detachment, as if observing them wryly and sometimes critically. How far do you agree with the observation below about Adcock's style, in relation to the group of poems you are studying?

> Adcock's ironic detachment works both for and against her. While it keeps sentimentality firmly in check and enables her to cultivate an appealing sense of unillusioned self-knowledge, it can also create too much distance between the poet and the experience or the objects in the poem. As a result of this distance, the impersonal tone of her earlier work is sometimes forced.
>
> (Tess Lewis, *PN Review*, March 1992)

Who reads these poems?
How do they interpret them?

The simple answer to the first question will be **you**. You will read and respond to a poem in a way that is individual, in a way that is governed by such things as your personality, your experience of life, earlier reading experiences, your views and attitudes towards issues, events and relationships – and much else besides. But, however personal your own response, which will make it subtly or obviously different from your peers, the range of responses among a group of you is not limitless – there will be connections and similarities between the ways you all respond. This is because any class or group of people who live, study or work together usually have some features in common: your age, a shared language, your gender, the area where you live, perhaps a similar upbringing or schooling, and/or experience of the same culture with its political system, mass media and so on. So, the way you read a poem is probably going to be very different from the way a young person from New York, or Cairo, or Peking would go about it.

The following activities suggest a range of ways for you to read, respond to and interpret the various poems and performance pieces in this collection. Largely, they encourage you to develop your own responses, ask where these might come from, and compare your readings with other students; but the last activity asks you to consider the readings of critics and journalists – who may have a rather different interpretation from your own.

✦ *Activities*
1 A poetry journal
Keep a journal which records your impressions of the poems and performance pieces you read. View your poetry journal as a kind of diary where you can note down feelings and thoughts

as they occur to you. It should provide plenty of ideas for coursework assignments later on. Your journal may contain:

- questions – about ideas, issues or language which you find puzzling and intriguing in the poems you read;
- feelings – about the language or subject matter of a poem: whether these make you feel amused, irritated, interested, upset, and so on;
- thoughts – about the ideas the poem gives you: whether it questions or develops your own thoughts on a given subject;
- memories – of past experiences which the poem has helped you to recall;
- comparisons – with other poems or stories you have read with similar subjects or use of language;
- judgements – on which poems you like or dislike, and why;
- analysis – of the way you have responded: aspects of your personal history, and of your reading experiences which make you respond in the way you do.

2 Reading poems aloud

One of the best ways of making sense of a poem, and of forming your own interpretation of it, is to experiment with ways of reading it aloud, especially in a small group. Choose a single poem, or perhaps a group of poems on a common subject, and, in groups, work out a way of performing these poems to an audience. In preparation, experiment by using all your voices, with different ways of reading the poem aloud. Aim to express the poem's voice, mood, subject matter and sound effects by:

- using contrasting voices – high/low: male/female;
- varying your reading speed – quickly/slowly;
- deciding when to use solo, pair or unison voices;
- varying the volume – soft/loud;
- adapting the rhythm – regular/irregular: smooth/broken;
- altering the tone of your voice – warm/cold: gentle/hard;
- varying your intonation – voice rising/falling.

3 Writing your own poems

Your response to a poem can be enhanced by drawing upon the inspiration it gives you to write a poem or creative piece of your own. The following are possible approaches:

a Alternative endings

Choose a longer poem such as Jackie Kay's *The Adoption Papers* (the last chapter), or Liz Lochhead's dramatic monologue 'Almost Miss Scotland' (p. 10), and imagine a different way in which the piece might end. Aim to write your version of the ending or final part of the piece in the same style and form as the original.

b Alternative personae

Choose any poem written in the voice of a character. Write a poem from the point of view of another character referred to in the original poem, which might serve as a reply or a response. For example, you might write as Barbra in Liz Lochhead's 'Favourite Shade' (p. 31), or as Mrs Tilscher in 'In Mrs Tilscher's Class' (p. 68).

c Dramatic opening lines

Use the first line of any poem which begins powerfully as a trigger for writing a poem about an alternative experience, real or imagined. For example, you might pick from Fleur Adcock:

- 'All my scars are yours.' ('Knife-play', p. 86);
- '"Will I die?" you ask.' ('For Andrew', p. 88).

4 Close reading

There are various ways you can go about reading a poem closely and making sense of it. Choose the approach which you feel will best make sense of the poem you are reading:

a By distinctive features

Poems often have one or more distinctive features about them – conveying a mood; telling a story; portraying a character; creating a clear, mental picture, or evoking impressions of sound, rhythm or music. Depending on the poem you are studying, choose one of the features in the list below, and highlight (perhaps with various colours of marker pens on a copy of the poem), all the words and phrase which convey different aspects of this:

- mood – for example, anger, love, sadness, disgust, ridicule;
- story – for example, features of narrative: narrator, plot, episodes, character, setting, message or moral;
- voice – the 'idiolect' of the speaker: the individual vocabulary, expressions, tone, speech rhythms of that character;
- imagery – strong images of a subject, perhaps in the form of similes and metaphors;
- sound effects – words or phrases which create sounds: strong rhythmic effects, use of rhyme.

Look over all the words you have highlighted and ask:

- which words or phrases might you group together?
- how would you label each group of words or phrases?
- what connections and what oppositions do you see in the groups of words and phrases you have marked?
- what insights has this process given you about the subject and the title of the poem?

b By literary analysis

On your own or in pairs, read your chosen poem carefully. Make notes on the following aspects of the poem:

- subject matter – what the poem is about;
- mood – the main feelings in the poem;
- voice – who is speaking; who is being addressed;
- form – free or formal verse: verse shape;
- style – line length and pattern; type of rhythm – conversational, musical, rap, use of metre; rhyme – mid or end-of-line; imagery – for example, metaphors, similes, personification.

For each aspect, aim to:

- describe – what the characteristics of the poem seem to be;
- explain – why they are there, and what effect they have;
- express – your feelings, reactions and thoughts about the poem;

- criticise – features of the language which work well or less well;
- deconstruct – the implicit meanings of the language which might reveal assumptions about class, gender or racial relationships in the poem;
- evaluate – how successful this poem is and how well it works for you.

5 Alternative readings

What kind of person might have written the following and where could it have been published?

About Liz Lochhead:

> But *True Confessions* and *New Clichés* underscores her talent as a humorist, sending up the female condition in a way that demonstrates her belief that not only are we all sisters under the skin, but that we screw up in remarkably similar fashion.

About Carol Ann Duffy:

> The poetry of Carol Ann Duffy consistently draws attention to the nature of language and the ways in which it constructs our relationship between ourselves and others. Language is not a series of transparent signs through which reality is perceived, but a structuring and differentiating system which constructs reality by reflecting the concerns of the social order which produced it. The task of the writer and the reader is to continually deconstruct linguistic signs in order to expose the ideological nature of their significations.

Write a review of a poem or group of poems from the collection from the point of view of a reader whose perspective and purpose for writing is likely to be very different from your own. Choose one of the following situations (or something similar):

- a female reviewer writing for *The Guardian*;
- a male reviewer writing for *The Sun*;
- a reviewer writing for a popular teenage magazine which includes book reviews;

- a reviewer for a radical; marxist; feminist; civil rights; or alternative magazine such as *Private Eye*.

In order to write this review convincingly, you may need to do some research into the nature of the publication you are writing for. Consider, for example, the publication's readership, its style of writing and mode of addressing readers, and its 'political' leanings if relevant.

6 Comparative activities

The following comment gives some suggestions for responding more formally to the collection of poetry as a whole, and for making comparisons between one poet or group of poems and another:

a   The greatest writers lay no stress upon sex one way or another. The critic is not reminded as he reads them that he belongs to the masculine or the feminine gender.

(Virginia Woolf, essay on Hemingway)

How far do you agree with this comment? Does it help you to assess the 'greatness' of the poets in this collection? Write an essay in which you discuss the value of this comment in relation to your study of two or more poets represented here.

(If you are interested in investigating Virginia Woolf's views on female writers further, begin with *A Room of One's Own*, CUP, 1995.)

b   I was a poet before I was a woman poet. I was writing poetry before I realised this was not something generally done by women. And I didn't think of myself as any different from a male poet, until I discovered I was.

(Fleur Adcock, *Acumen*, 1992)

How important is it that poetry by women should be expressing issues of female concern? Discuss your own attitudes to poetry by women, by drawing upon any of the following points:

- that women may write about subjects differently from men, and draw upon different viewpoints;
- that women writers 'have an obligation to write about important experiences like giving birth' (Fleur Adcock) in order to make public the female experience;
- that there should be anthologies for women's poetry;
- that some bookshops have special sections for women's poetry.

c To a certain extent, all four poets in this collection explore issues of identity – defined, amongst other things, by race, country, gender and class. By referring closely to the work of two or more of the poets represented here, compare the differing ways in which they have presented and expressed their subjects. Which poem has had the most impact on you?

◆

GLOSSARY

Liz Lochhead

'Almost Miss Scotland'

3   **stramash:** uproar, commotion

7   **skinnymalinky:** a thin, skinny person

15   **tapselteerie:** topsy-turvey

15   **peerie:** stiletto

46   **plooks:** pimples; spots

52   **heuchter-choochter:** a Gaelic speaking Highlander, but with overtones here of a person unfamiliar with the ways of the big city; rather provincial

54   **bubblyjock:** turkey cock

95   **oaxters:** arm-pits

'The Alternative ... Part One'

55   **Jezebel:** infamous wife of Ahab, King of Israel; also used to describe a sexually 'loose' woman

56   **Delilah:** a beautiful but treacherous woman, from the story of Samson and Delilah in the Old Testament of the Bible

57   **Mary Magdalen:** patron saint of penitents, being herself a reformed prostitute and friend of Jesus, in the New Testament of the Bible

65   **siren:** one of the mythical monsters, half woman and half bird, who sang so alluringly that they caused sailors to become distracted and steer their ships on to the rocks

67   **Medusa:** one of the three Gorgons, whose heads had snakes for hair, and who turned anyone who looked at them to stone
      Medea: in classical mythology, she helped Jason of the Argonauts to obtain the golden fleece; also used to describe a sorceress

69   **Delphic sybil:** a prophetess of Apollo. Delphi in ancient Greece had a temple of Apollo, famous for its oracle, who was consulted for advice

'View of Scotland/Love Poem'

2   **Hogmanay:** in Scotland, the last day of the year

6   **sockeye:** blue-backed salmon of Alaska

'Renfield's Nurse'

5   **huckaback:** stout linen or cotton fabric with rough surface, for towels, etc.

'Good Wood'

8   **gean:** fruit of the wild cherry

23   **shillelagh:** Irish cudgel of blackthorn or oak

28   **marquetry:** inlaid work in wood, ivory, etc.

'Six Men Monologues'

No. 4 Kimberley

77   **dulep:** normally 'julep'; a sweet drink taken as a mask for medicine

No. 5 Mo

108 **Kelvinside:** a 'posh' part of Glasgow; so an indication of how 'well-spoken' people say 'crash'

'Favourite Shade'

6   **Dreich:** dreary; dull

Jackie Kay

The Adoption Papers

128 **Paul Robeson:** (1898–1976) black actor and singer, also campaigned for black civil rights

131 **Burns:** (1759–96) Robert Burns, a celebrated Scottish poet, remembered on Burns Night, held on 29 January each year

133 **Shelley:** Percy Bysshe Shelley (1792–1822), a Romantic poet

Chapter 4: **Baby Lazarus:** alluding to the man Jesus raised from the dead in the Bible story; also a leper or beggar

228 **Book of Job:** book in the Old Testament of the Bible about a man who personified patience in the face of adversity

344 **Donny Osmond:** child pop star famous in the 1970s
David Cassidy: also a pop star famous in the 1970s, adored by teenagers of the day

345 **Starsky and Hutch:** a very popular American TV detective serial in the 1970s, which attracted a large teenage audience

347 **Pearl Bailey:** (1918–90) an American black jazz singer

349 **Bessie Smith:** (1894–1937) an American black jazz singer and songwriter, known as the 'Empress of the Blues'

Chapter 7:   Black Bottom: a ballroom dance along with the 'cha cha'

430 *The Prime of Miss Jean Brodie:* novel by Muriel Spark, about a respectable girls' school in Edinburgh in the 1960s.

446 **Angela Davis:** a black American communist, who at 26, was wrongfully imprisoned (and later acquitted) for kidnapping, conspiracy and murder

476 **Roseberries:** Julius (1918–53) and Ethel Rosenberg (1915–53) were Americans who were executed for espionage activities on behalf of Russia

613 **Adam Carrington:** character in *Dynasty*, a famous American soap opera during the 1980s

676 **blether:** chatter too much or foolishly

Carol Ann Duffy

'Comprehensive'

14   **Masjid:** Mosque

27   **Ejaz:** boy's name

'War Photographer'

6   **Belfast. Beirut. Phnom Penh:** cities where war and terrible carnage have taken place for religious or political reasons

'In Mrs Tilscher's Class'

11   **Brady and Hindley:** Ian Brady and Myra Hindley, known as the 'Moors Murderers' of several children in the 1960s, and still serving life imprisonment

'Making Money'

5   *niyariwallah*: person who sifts drains for lost coins, etc

26   **Bergama:** town in Turkey, on the west coast

'We Remember Your Childhood Well'

5   *Film Fun:* a comic containing cartoon strips of humorous films

'Welltread'

9   **Aberfan:** a coal-mining village in South Wales. In 1966, a landslide from a slag heap engulfed part of the village, including the school, with the loss of 144 lives, including 116 children.

'The Good Teachers'

6   **South Sea Bubble:** a famous incident quoted in English school history books. This was the speculative mania associated with the South Sea Trading Company, which ended disastrously with the financial ruin of many people who had invested in the company.

      Defenestration of Prague: another famous incident quoted in school history books. In the 16th century, two Roman Catholic leaders were thrown out of a window at the castle of Prague by two Protestants. The men landed in the moat and sustained only minor injuries.

Fleur Adcock

'Knife Play'
36   **Pyrrhic:** a victory won at too heavy a price, like the costly victory won by Pyrrhus in 279 BC. Pyrrhus lost all his best officers and many soldiers.

'Bogyman'
45   *Ambit*: name of a current poetry magazine

'The Inner Harbour'
     Paua-Shell: large, edible New Zealand shellfish
     Cat's-Eye: precious stone of Sri Lanka and Malabar

'On the Land'
17   **Candlemas:** feast of the Virgin Mary, when candles are blessed (2 February)

'Chippenham'
39   **impetigo:** contagious pustular disease of the skin

'Mary Magdalene and the Birds'
     Mary Magdalene: see Liz Lochhead's 'The Alternative – Part One' on page 139

FURTHER READING

Poetry

Liz Lochhead

Dreaming Frankenstein and Collected Poems (Polygon Books, 1984)
True Confessions and New Clichés (Polygon Books, 1985)
Bagpipe Muzak (Penguin, 1991)

Jackie Kay

The Adoption Papers (Bloodaxe Books, 1991)
Two's Company (Blackie, 1992: a book of children's poetry)
Other Lovers (Bloodaxe Books, 1993)

Carol Ann Duffy

Standing Female Nude (1985); *Selling Manhattan* (1987); *The Other Country* (1990); *Mean Time* (1993). All Anvil Press Poetry.

Fleur Adcock

Tigers (1967); *High Tide in the Garden* (1971); *The Scenic Route* (1974); *The Inner Harbour* (1979); *The Incident Book* (1986); *Time Zones* (1991). All Oxford University Press.

Plays and TV work

Liz Lochhead

Tartuffe (Polygon, 1985: a rhyming translation/adaptation of Molière's play)
Mary Queen of Scots Got Her Head Chopped Off (Penguin, 1989)
Dracula (Penguin, 1989)

Jackie Kay

Chiaroscuro (1986) and *Twice Over* (1988): plays presented by Gay Sweatshop.
Twice Through the Heart (poetry documentary for BBC2)